MW00620656

Hoodoo Spiritual Baths

Cleansing Conjure
with
Washes and Waters

by Aura Laforest

Lucky Mojo Curio Company
Forestville, California

✦ 2014 ✦

Hoodoo Spiritual Baths:
Cleansing Conjure with Washes and Waters
© 2014 Aura Laforest

Text:
Aura Laforest

Art:
Charles C. Dawson, Charles M. Quinlan, Karen the Graphics Fairy, K. Rudin,

Cover:
Unknown Valmor Artist, Charles C. Dawson, Greywolf Townsend

Editor:
catherine yronwode

Production:
nagasiva yronwode, catherine yronwode, Greywolf Townsend

Illustrations:
Baths and Floor Washes, 1934 - 2014   13
Circa 1890 Bath Tub and Shower Combination   21

Selections from the following previously published material is used by permission: "Hoodoo in Theory and Practice" by catherine yronwode at LuckyMojo.com/hoodoo.html © 1994-2013 catherine yronwode; "Hoodoo Herb and Root Magic" by catherine yronwode © 2004 catherine yronwode; "Southern Spirits" at Southern-Spirits.com © 2004 catherine yronwode; "The Lucky Mojo Free Spells Archive" LuckyMojo.com/spells.html © 1994-2013 catherine yronwode; Lucky Mojo Curio Company Forum at Forum.LuckyMojo.com © 2008-2013 The Lucky Mojo Curio Co.; Momma Starr's Uncrossing Bath and Cleansing Floor Sprinkle © 2014 Starr Casas; Madame Nadia's Gold Digger Body Scrub © 2014 Nadia Potter; "Hoodoo Honey and Sugar Spells" by Deacon Millett © 2013 Fred Burke.

First Edition 2014

Published by
The Lucky Mojo Curio Company
6632 Covey Road
Forestville, California 95436
LuckyMojo.com

ISBN-10: 0-9719612-6-3 / ISBN-13: 978-0-9719612-6-5

Printed in Canada.

CONTENTS

DEDICATION

To the little one within that made this book possible,
may I measure up as a mother once you're without.

ACKNOWLEDGEMENTS

This book would never have come to be without the seed planted many months ago by catherine yronwode as we chatted together before a reading. My sincerest thanks to her and to nagasiva yronwode for their support, technical help, and knowledge throughout the writing process. You have taught me to be discerning and respectful of the history and roots of hoodoo as well as of those who created it. Without the information and teachings available as a result of your work, Miss cat, rootwork would not be the increasingly popular practice it is today, nor would I be writing about it now.

My grateful thanks to Momma Starr, Madame Nadia, Deacon Millett, and Miss cat yronwode for kindly allowing some of their previously published bath-spells to be reproduced within these pages, and to Miss Michaele, Papa Newt, and Miss Tammie Lee for contributing material as well.

Thanks also to the members of the Lucky Mojo Forum who provided the questions which make up much of this book and the curiosity which helps spur on and improve everyone's practice in magic and life! As I daily read the questions that come in and the answers provided by my fellow Forum Moderator team members, I am humbled by the variety, complexity, and beauty that make up the base of conjure and the skill of my fellow practitioners.

Finally, a special mention goes to the members of the Association of Independent Readers and Rootworkers (AIRR) who have contributed their knowledge and advice to this book:

catherine yronwode	Dr. Johannes
ConjureMan Ali	Lukianos
Deacon Millett	Miss Bri
Devi Spring	Leah Rivera
Momma Starr	Madame Nadia
Miss Michaele	Mary Bee

HOODOO, A BIT OF BACKGROUND

Hoodoo, also known as conjure, rootwork, tricking, or helping yourself, is a system of folk magic developed in America by the African slaves who were sold and exploited here and by their descendants. Like the people who first forged the work and have become an integral part of the American cultural fabric, hoodoo still thrives today and it has come to be appreciated by many people raised outside of black American culture.

At its genesis, hoodoo drew from African homeland cultures, but early on practitioners began to include admixtures of European and Native American herbology and magic, set within the context of Protestant Christianity, the dominant religion of the United States. Most practitioners are Christian — primarily Baptist — and much of the work is done with prayer, Bible in hand.

With emancipation and urbanization, conjure workers gradually gained access to the wide variety of herbs and prepared supplies that became available with the development of the mail order industry. By the late 19th and early 20th centuries, influences from Jewish and German-American folk magic and from religions like Spiritualism, the New Thought Movement, and Catholicism were adopted to varying degrees by practitioners who were exposed to them or sought them out by ordering books from which to learn.

It is important to note that working roots is not a religion per se, but a practice and an art, much like cooking, sewing, and cabinet-making are. The goals of the work are magical and pragmatic, and are intended to better situations in the home, for the family, on the job, and within the community. Home practitioners make use of materials available locally and via mail order, and they employ simple techniques that are accessible to all and can be customized to suit the situation. Work may also be performed by engaging professional conjure doctors, who are paid for their services.

Hoodoo is an evolving tradition and world-wide interest in it has blossomed via the internet. However, as always, it remains the folk magic of the African American community, deeply rooted in Southern culture.

Read more about the history of hoodoo online at

LuckyMojo.com/hoodoohistory.html
Southern-Spirits.com

Read more about the history of hoodoo in these books:

"Hoodoo Herb and Root Magic" by catherine yronwode
"The Art of Hoodoo Candle Magic" by catherine yronwode

SPIRITUAL SUPPLIES

During most of the 19th century, most rural root doctors and hoodoo practitioners hand-crafted the spiritual supplies they used in their practices. Many of the roots, herbs, and curios chosen and prayed over were wildcrafted as needed to address specific situations. In addition, common household and farm goods were widely used to create hand-made supplies.

As a result of increasing urbanization, people came to have less access to the areas in which roots and herbs grow and so, from the early 1900s onward, supplies for doing a job were often purchased from a local general store, pharmacy, or spiritual supply house. In the 1920s, pharmacies that carried herbs and other materials for use in conjure came to be called "hoodoo drugstores." There were many such retail outlets in cities like Memphis, Atlanta, Chicago, Saint Louis, and Baltimore. Practitioners in smaller towns did not travel to obtain supplies; rather, they made use of the mail order departments of herbalists, cosmetics companies, hoodoo drugstores, and spiritual suppliers who advertised in black-owned newspapers like the *Chicago Defender* and shipped their products nationwide via postal mail. These companies came to be known in the South as "order houses."

Hoodoo drugstores and order houses were not the first to develop standard recipes to address specific conditions — terms such as Hot Foot and Goofer Dust can be found in 19th century accounts of hoodoo — but as practitioner-merchants proliferated from the 1920s through the 1960s, they did develop the custom of naming baths, perfumes, oils, sachet powders, and incenses for the conditions to be remedied. Thus "Fear Not to Walk Over Evil" products protect against foot-track magic while "Look Me Over" products garner attention to oneself or to articles dressed with them.

Read more about hoodoo drugstores and order houses in this book:
"Spiritual Merchants" by Carolyn Morrow Long
Read more about hoodoo drugstores and order houses online at
Southern-Spirits.com/anon-dr-pearce-saint-louis.html
Southern-Spirits.com/anon-hoodoo-in-detroit.html
Southern-Spirits.com/byrd-bichons-drugstore-houston.html
LuckyMojo.com/luckybrown.html
LuckyMojo.com/cloverhorn.html
LuckyMojo.com/luckyheart.html
LuckyMojo.com/luckymongol.html

- **Herbs, Roots, Minerals, and Zoological Curios:** Natural curios are the foundation of conjure. Herbal, mineral, and zoological mixtures are used to create condition-oriented spiritual supply product lines. Read more about hoodoo herbs, roots, and minerals online at **Herb-Magic.com**
- **Essential, Synthetic, and Fragrance Oils:** Scents are added to spiritual supplies to create recognizable aromas and to enhance magical effects. Read more about essential, synthetic, and fragrance oils online at **LuckyMojo.com/essentialoils.html**
- **Condition Oils:** Also called dressing or anointing oils, these formulas blend herbs and scents in skin-safe carrier oils for use as body perfumes and to anoint candles, feed mojo bags, and fix oil-resistant objects. Read more about hoodoo anointing oils online at **LuckyMojo.com/oils.html**
- **Condition Incenses:** These combine the formula's roots, herbs, and signature scent with an incense base. Incense is used to perfume the air and waft one's desires through a location and/or the mind. Read more about hoodoo incenses online at **LuckyMojo.com/incense.html**
- **Condition Sachet Powders:** Roots and herbs with the formula's scent in a neutral powder base are dusted on paperwork, added to toiletry powders, and mixed with local dirt for deployment. Read more about hoodoo sachets online at **LuckyMojo.com/powders.html**
- **Condition Bath Crystals:** The formula's scent and herbs are blended in a mineral bath salt base which can be dissolved in water for spiritual bathing or to create customized floor-washes or laundry liquids. Read more about hoodoo bath crystals online at **LuckyMojo.com/baths.html**
- **Washes and Spiritual Soaps:** Spiritual supplies made in a soapy base include Chinese Wash, Black & White Soap, and Florida Water Soap. Read more about spiritual soaps online at **LuckyMojo.com/soaps.html**
- **Colognes, Toilet Waters, and Perfumes:** Scents in an alcohol base are used directly on the body or splashed into baths and floor washes. Read more about spiritual perfumes online at **LuckyMojo.com/perfumes.html**

BASIC CONJURE TERMINOLOGY AND PRACTICES

• **Hoodoo, Conjure, Witchcraft, Rootwork**: African American folk magic is also known as doing a job, hoodooing, tricking, conjuring, working roots, putting down (or cleaning up) a mess, throwing for someone, helping yourself, witchcrafting, and using that stuff.

• **Practitioner, Client, Target**: The person doing the job is a practitioner or, if professional, a root doctor, rootworker, advisor, spiritual worker, or conjure doctor. The person being helped is the client. A person who is unknowingly being worked upon is the target.

• **The Doctrine of Signatures**: This magical theory holds that as a thing — particularly a curio from nature — appears, tastes, or feels, so shall it affect the condition or person on which it is used.

• **Dressing, Anointing, Loading, Fixing, Preparing**: These are methods of readying people, animals, foot tracks, shoes, clothing, bedding, housewares, furniture, and food. Dressing and anointing are surface applications; loading is internal; fixing and preparing are general terms that include the above, plus prayer, smoking in incense, and washing.

• **Contact Magic, Foot-Track Magic**: The target comes into direct contact with a curio or item that has been magically fixed or prepared.

• **Sympathetic Magic**: The worker establishes a magical link between a part of someone, such as their hair, nails, photo, name, or other personal concerns, and their whole: What is done to the part will affect the whole.

• **Bible Magic**: Portions of scripture are recited, inscribed on candles, written in petitions, dissolved into liquids for bathing and ingestion, or burnt to ash for use in spells. The Bible is also used in divination.

• **Working with Spirits**: Allies from the spirit world may include Biblical figures, family ancestors, crossroads spirits, persons known for having excelled at certain activities while alive, wild animals, and beloved pets.

• **Container Spells**: Spells are often performed within sealed spaces, whose many forms include honey jars, sugar bowls, vinegar bottles, home freezers, flower pots, mojo bags, doll-babies, and mirror boxes.

• **Candle Magic**: Candles are employed to send spiritual influences into the world or to receive information about those at a distance.

• **Baths and Teas**: Liquids assist in cleansing, protection, luck-drawing, and obtaining love or success. They may be self-administered, prescribed by a root doctor, or given to a client by a hands-on spiritual healer.

CLEANING THE HOME AND THE BODY

Throughout the world indigenous and tribal people have originated various forms of cleansing rituals to restore purity, prepare for prayer, and soothe the soul from affliction. Major contemporary religions such as Hinduism, Buddhism, Shinto, Judaism, Christianity, and Islam also include such purification practices, each making use of special waters and prescribed techniques for their application.

Cleansing the home and bathing the body are foundational practices of hoodoo as well. They are the everyday spiritual jobs that, although easily done, help keep life running smoothly and allow practitioners to avoid problems setting in and sticking around. We consider it perfectly normal to wash our physical selves and premises on a regular basis as part of our personal hygiene. Spiritual hygiene can be considered in the same way!

If you can take a shower or mop your floor, you can take a spiritual bath or do a spiritual house cleaning. The practices are accessible to anyone, even those with only modest magical gifts. These mundane activities may not have the glamour of an elaborate candle spell, but the greatest effectiveness often arises in simplicity, and cleaning spells are simple and strong.

Learning to properly wash the body and home are essential skills for any magical practitioner. When performed regularly, cleanings tend to keep the jealousy, negative energy, and crossed conditions of others at bay. They can also provide strong protection from unexpected spiritual attacks. Anyone meeting or dealing with the public on a regular basis will benefit from spiritual bathing for these and other reasons.

Over time and with practice, the work becomes second-nature and is easily integrated into daily life. A capful of Chinese Wash in the mop buckets and laundry, praying as you sweep, cleaning from back to front, taking an herbal bath before sunrise on Mondays to start the week off right. These and other simple conjure practices can ease social tensions in the home, making it a welcoming and happy place in which to spend time. Additionally, when you become spiritual clean, you will find that others feel comfortable befriending you and spending time in your presence.

Cleansing and bathing practices, both mundane and magical, have measurable long-term influence on the quality of life when used regularly, and thus the importance of making them a part of household routine cannot be stressed enough.

HOUSE CLEANING AND BATHING FOR SPECIFIC PURPOSES

Now, you may think that bathing and cleaning are primarily undertaken to cleanse the home or person, but in fact they have further uses. Love baths enhance marital life, money drawing washes bring in prosperity, and healing baths may remediate spiritual ills. Baths can be used to influence others or even to curse. As you develop a deep connection with hoodoo culture, you will find a wide array of reasons to incorporate spiritual baths into your work.

- **Uncrossing and Protection from Evil:** The same bath products that are used to clear off evil from a person can also be diluted into wash waters for clothes and mop waters for the floors. This is done in order to protect the home and to shield family members from spiritual attack.
- **To Draw in Love, Money, Blessings, Luck, or Health:** Spiritual baths may be used alone or as preparation for more elaborate spells. Drawing work usually begins with a bath; house cleansing is optional. Some people bathe again at the conclusion of the work. Others prefer to bathe or wash up every day throughout an ongoing spell of drawing work.
- **Ruling and Controlling:** Influencing or dominating others in the home or on the job can be accomplished with baths, but it is more common to achieve such ends through laundering the clothes of family members or by a prescriptive domination floor wash of the home or workplace.
- **Cursing and Crossing:** A full spiritual bath is usually performed at the conclusion of cursing spells to ask for forgiveness and cleanse the body and soul from sin. Throughout a long term job of crossing, such as after a daily activity like shaking a vinegar jar or burning a black candle, a spiritual hand wash will keep the hands and work space cleansed.

HIRING A HANDS-ON SPIRITUAL WORKER

Hoodoo is not a secret form of magic and there are few, if any, "solitary practitioners" because it is a living part of African American culture. Fortune telling, spell-casting, and spiritual cleansing are openly offered to clients by professional root doctors. If you live near such a worker, you may arrange for a hands-on bath, foot wash, head cleansing, or hand blessing, or hire a helper to come to your home or business to perform a spiritual cleaning on the premises. Good hands-on workers are well worth the prices they charge.

HOW OFTEN AND HOW LONG

Those who are new to the practice of rootwork often ask how long and how often baths or house cleansings should be undertaken. Many also want to know how great a part these activities play in the overall tradition of conjure. However, as tempting as it may be to supply you with an answer, the truth is that questions like "How often?" and "How long?" do not have singular or uniform answers, even among long-time practitioners.

Many workers only take spiritual baths or perform spiritual house-cleanings on an as-needed basis, such as when they have been under magical attack; the rest of the time they simply tidy up and stay positive.

Others like to incorporate spiritual bathing and house cleaning into their regular maintenance program of cleanliness. They choose to substitute spiritual supply products for mundane household cleaners whenever possible.

Some spell-casters are not interested in deep or frequent cleansings per se, but they do like to begin every single conjure job with a brief bath or at least a hand wash, in order to enter into the work in a righteous manner.

Other practitioners prefer to seek out local healers to administer hands-on baths, foot washes, or cleansings to them, and find satisfaction in doing so.

When consulting with a root doctor, you may be told to repeat your baths, whether for jinx breaking or for good luck, for a certain number of days in a row, such as 3, 7, or 13. You may also be told to repeat the baths according to a frequency pattern, such as 3 times a week for 3 weeks, at the first crescent Moon, on the first day of each month, or at every menstrual cycle. You may be advised to perform house cleanings periodically as well, with timings such as the first day of each month or once a year, and to augment them (or not) with weekly or monthly washes to attract what you desire.

A root doctor who prescribes a certain number and/or frequency of baths to you may be making a determination based on the type of work and how long standing your situation is. For example, a person with a good life and an optimistic outlook may be fine with a single uncrossing bath, repeated 3 to 4 times a year, while a person who has suffered a long run of bad luck and difficult circumstances would want to consider a full 13-day course of cleansing baths followed by a monthly or even a weekly bath thereafter.

To integrate house cleaning, baths, and teas into your conjure practice, start simple, ask questions, assess your results, and develop further as you see fit. There is very little that can go wrong with a bath, so relax and enjoy it!

PREPARATION: TERMINOLOGY AND TECHNIQUES

Preparing the water for a floor wash or spiritual bath is similar to pouring a regular bath or brew strong tea — sometimes a combination of both! The differences will lie in the ingredients used, the magical purpose of the activities, and the prayers and actions surrounding the bathing experience.

• **Infusion:** To make enough herb tea for a full bathtub, bring 4 cups of water to a boil, turn off the heat, and add 4-6 tablespoons of loose herbs. For a pour-over bath, use 1 tablespoon of herb mixture per cup of water. Allow the mixture to steep, covered, for the prescribed amount of time. This method of preparation is known as infusion.

• **Decoction:** If your bath consists mostly of roots or barks, it will be more difficult to draw their essence into the water. Add woody botanicals to the water before you begin heating it and simmer everything together the prescribed amount of time. This technique is known as decoction.

• **Dissolving Mineral Crystals:** Mineral bath crystals can be dissolved directly into a bathtub or into a pot of hot water. Placing them in a small muslin sack before dropping them in the bath saves on bathtub scrubbing, as does dissolving them as you infuse or decoct a bath-tea.

• **Straining, Skimming, and Decanting:** You may remove spent herbs by straining the bath-tea through cheese cloth or with a metal strainer. If your bath contains materials that sink to the bottom, pour off the liquid and leave the solids behind; this is called decanting. If some portions float, skim them off with a slotted spoon and decant the remainder.

• **Diluting:** Either add the bath-tea to a full tub of warm water for a soaking bath (sitting in the tub) or dilute it with a gallon of water for a pour-over bath (pouring it over your head and body).

• **Ingestion:** If your herb bath is safe for consumption, you may also use it to prepare a cup of tea to drink. If your herb bath contains materials that are toxic to drink or you have added essential oils or minerals to it, then choose a different herb tea to support your intentions. DO NOT dissolve bath crystals into tea. They will render the brew undrinkable.

• **Prayer:** As you prepare ingredients, take a bath, scrub the premises, or drink a tea, you may recite portions of scripture suited to your condition or express your own heartfelt prayer, desire, wish, or command. Your faith-filled words will infuse and diffuse within the water.

Spiritual Baths and Floor Washes, 1934 - 2014. Art by Charles C. Dawson, Charles M. Quinlan, R. C. Adams, K. Rudin, and Two Unknown Artists for Famous Products, Oracle Products, R.C. Adams, Clover Horn, and Standard O & B Supply.

SPIRITUAL HOUSE CLEANING

Cleaning house in a spiritual manner may be done separately from, or combined with, regular house cleaning activities. In hoodoo, there are traditional precedents for doing the work either way.

The first time a home or space is being cleansed, or if a place is very crossed up or feels haunted, you may do a spiritual cleaning on the already washed house, paying special attention to all the corners, walls, and floors.

When a longstanding negative condition is being taken off a person, you may begin with a spiritual bath for the affected party and then add some of the bath water to the scrub water used for the home or business cleaning.

After the initial cleaning, spiritual washes may become a maintenance chore or regular practice. In other words, if the place you're working on is already in good shape spiritually, you just want to make sure it stays that way.

Washes to bring in blessings, money, or love may be done on their own, or following a cleansing. Use prosperity washes throughout the house, on the sidewalk and steps leading up to a shop, or in any room where business is conducted. Peaceful home washes work well in the kitchen, dining room, and living room. Love drawing washes generally lead right to the bedroom.

Floor washes influence those who walk upon the floors. Historically, after emancipation from slavery, many African Americans went into domestic labour. This presented the opportunity to fix mop water with spiritual supplies like Essence of Bend-Over, for better treatment from employers. To this day, some hotels and cleaning services add conjure products like Chinese Wash to their scrub water, because "clients like the way it smells."

Brooms are associated with a rich history of folkloric practices. When moving into a new home, leave the old broom behind, buy a new one, and use it to sweep the premises from back to front to rid yourself of any trouble left by the previous occupants. Buying a new broom also prevents your own past problems from following you from the old house to the new one.

Many folks won't sweep in the kitchen once the Sun has set, for to do so would sweep away the household's luck and money. A broom can also be used to sweep away unwanted people, either by leaning it across the door during the day or by sweeping behind folks as they leave. Turning a broom up and dusting it with salt and pepper will send folks away too. And don't sweep people's feet with a broom: You could send them to jail or condemn them to childlessness or spinsterhood.

HOUSE CLEANING IN SEVEN EASY STEPS

Follow these basic steps to perform a spiritual house cleaning:

1. Tidy and sweep: After tidying up so that you have easy access to the floors and walls, sweep each room in turn. Considering the house as a whole, work from top to bottom and also from back to front to get rid of crossed conditions or from front to back to draw in good conditions. The reason to work top-to-bottom is purely practical: If you sweep the floor first, dust or junk from the ceiling will fall down and mess up the clean floor. Unless the home or place of business is new, you do not need a new broom.

2. Prepare the wash water: To a bucket of fresh, hot water add either a couple of tablespoons of Chinese Wash, a prepared herbal bath-tea, or a small amount of mineral bath and floor wash crystals. If desired, you may use your regular commercial floor cleaning solutions with an added drop of condition oil or essential oil instead. You may need several buckets if the house is large, so keep your materials on hand to refill the bucket.

3. Scrub each room in turn: Within each room, work from top to bottom and also from back to front for cleansing or from front to back for drawing. Pray from the heart or from the Bible as you work: Psalms 23 is a good choice. Pay special attention to the front stoop or doorstep.

4. Don't forget the walls: Spritz your cleaning water mix onto a Swiffer-type mop (the flat kind with an adjustable-angle head) and run it down the walls. If the walls are covered with a paint or wallpaper that is sensitive to washing, use a sponge to lightly go over them.

5. Clean the floor: Hardwood floors should be mopped with the cleaning solution. Carpeted floors can be cleansed by spraying them lightly with a diluted solution of your scrub water. This can be done by using a steam-cleaner with some of your spiritual supplies added, or by laying down and then vacuuming up a dry floor sprinkle made with herbs and/or mineral salts.

6. Finish each room with a prayer: Light a white candle in each room as you finish it and leave. Say a short prayer as you light the candle. To save on candles, you can work with inexpensive birthday candles or tea lights, or carry one candle from room to room, or just say the prayer.

7. Dispose of the scrub water: Throw the used scrub water off your property. If you live in an apartment, you may keep a cup of the water to throw into a crossroads and dispose of the rest down the drain as usual.

FLOOR WASHES

Any bath crystals or herbal blends prepared for spiritual bathing can be used as floor washes, but some are more popular with workers than others. Products often used in mop water for the house and home include:

- **Buffalo Ammonia:** Used in very small quantities to strip away crossed conditions and turn things around.
- **Chinese Wash:** To clear away evil messes and crossed conditions; to change bad luck to good and sorrow to joy.
- **Fear Not to Walk Over Evil Bath Crystals:** To protect against foot-track magic or tricks laid on the ground.
- **Fiery Wall of Protection Bath Crystals:** To provide strong, hot protection against all forms of physical and spiritual evil.
- **Hot Foot Crystal Salts:** Used as a sneaky trick to get an unwanted house-guest, renter, or family member to pack up and leave.
- **Holy Water:** To purify or sanctify a room or altar space.
- **House Blessing Bath Crystals:** To bless the home and family with happiness, health, and prosperity.
- **Jinx Killer Bath Crystals:** To remove a jinx, hex, or crossed conditions.
- **Money House Blessing Bath Crystals:** To keep the home prosperous; combines well with Money Stay With Me and Prosperity products.
- **Pine-Sol:** Similar to Chinese Wash, but scented with pine.
- **Peace Water:** To bring peace and friendship to any shared space; it is a two-part liquid and is shaken up before use.
- **Uncrossing Bath Crystals:** To remove a jinx, hex, or crossed conditions; to get rid of bad luck and left over spiritual effects of having been placed in difficult and unpleasant situations.
- **Van Van Bath Crystals:** To change bad luck to good; this product is similar to Chinese Wash, but it is not soapy or sudsy.
- **War Water:** To bring conflict and discord to any shared space.
- **13-Herb Bath:** An herb mix used much like Uncrossing Bath Crystals.

Read more about the history and use of specific washes online at
LuckyMojo.com/chinesewash.html
LuckyMojo.com/peacewater.html
LuckyMojo.com/warwater.html

BUSINESS DRAWING FLOOR WASH

In a bucket of mop water, combine a few drops of your first urine of the day, 9 drops of Money Drawing oil, and 3 tablespoons of Chinese Wash.

LUCKY BUSINESS SIDEWALK SCRUB WITH AMMONIA

Prepare a bucket of sidewalk scrub-water with a capful of ammonia, plus Cinnamon powder, and sugar. Pray Psalms 100 as you scrub.

TO KEEP AWAY THE LAW WHILE STIMULATING TRADE

(from *Hoodoo Herb and Root Magic* by catherine yronwode)
Mix 1 tablespoon each of Bergamot, Cloves, and Cedar oils in a bucket of water. Scrub out the front door and onto the sidewalk to drive off intruders. Make a second wash with Cinnamon oil, your own urine, and sugar. Scrub back from the sidewalk into the building to draw trade in.

LOVE DRAWING BEDROOM FLOOR WASH

Brew together dried Rose petals, Juniper berries, and Damiana leaf. Strain and add to a mop bucket of hot water; use in the bedroom only.

HOT FOOT FLOOR WASH FOR BAD GUESTS OR RENTERS

To move someone out, add 1 tablespoon Hot Foot Crystal Salts to mop water, mop only the target's bedroom, and pray Psalms 70 as you work.

HOME CLEANSING FLOOR WASH #1

This floor wash is both physically and spiritually cleansing. To a bucket of hot water add 1/4 cup Pine-Sol, 1 capful Chinese Wash, and 13 drops Pine oil or turpentine. Wash from back to front, praying Psalms 23.

HOME CLEANSING FLOOR WASH #2

This floor wash is also good for windows and glass surfaces. To a mop bucket of hot water add 1 cup white vinegar, 1 cup Lemongrass or Pine needle tea, and 1 pinch kosher salt. Pray Psalms 23 and 91 while working.

HOME CLEANSING FLOOR WASH #3

This floor wash keeps the home happy, cleansed, and blessed. To a mop-bucket full of hot water add 1/4 cup Pine-Sol, 1 capful Chinese Wash, and a few drops each of House Blessing and Peaceful Home condition oils.

FIXING THE LAUNDRY

Another traditional way to integrate the use of bath crystals, herbal teas, or special waters in daily household activities is when doing laundry. Laundry can be fixed for almost any magical purpose, from love to destruction, and the work can be done openly or as a sneaky trick in secret. Just add a pinch of diluted bath crystals, a cap of Chinese Wash, a bit of herbal tea, or left-over personal bathing water directly to the load of laundry. Although this can be done anytime during the wash cycle, waiting until the final rinse is most common.

Rather than adding the spiritual products directly to each load of laundry, some people prefer to pre-mix them into their dry or liquid laundry detergent or liquid fabric softener. If using liquid detergent, a small amount of bath crystals diluted in water, condition oil, herb tea, or fixed bath water can be added to the bottle and thoroughly mixed in.

An old-fashioned way of fixing laundry is to sprinkle a dilute solution of spiritual bath crystals or herbal tea on the dry clothes, using a laundry sprinkler, prior to ironing or pressing them.

- **Socks and Underwear:** Although any clothing can be fixed, it is best to work on socks and underwear that will be worn by the target. The clothing affected will be in direct contact with the skin. With socks, this acts as contact magic, but it is also a form of foot-track magic.
- **Bed Linens:** When working for passion and fidelity, fix bed sheets by laundering them with bath crystals or herb teas for love, sex, and peace in the home. Children's bed sheets can be prepared in the same way for protection, respect of parental authority, and success in studies.
- **Floor Mats and Towels:** Bathroom floor mats, hand towels, bath towels, curtains, and living room throws all benefit from being laundered with a bit of herbal tea or bath crystals for a peaceful home and prosperity. This method is a great way to avoid fights and encourage good relations with the in-laws when they come to visit!
- **Dishwashing:** The same blending methods used for fixing laundry products can be used for fixing dishwashing liquids. Be sure to rise well.
- **Personal Toiletry Supplies:** Personal washing and bathing products such as shampoo, body wash, or liquid hand soap can be fixed in the same way. They can then be used in the home or given as gifts to family, lovers, and co-workers, depending on their intended use.

LAUNDRY WASH TO BRING IN THE MONEY

During the rinse cycle of the laundry (preferably when washing a load of socks and underwear) add 1/2 cup of hot water into which you have dissolved a pinch each of Prosperity, Crown of Success, and Pay Me bath crystals. For help on the job, add a pinch of Steady Work to the blend.

LAUNDRY WASH TO CURB EXCESSIVE SPENDING

Add to the laundry 1/2 cup of hot water into which you have dissolved a pinch each of Money Stay With Me, King Solomon Wisdom, and Cast Off Evil bath crystals.

LAUNDRY WASH FOR GOOD SEX

(from *Hoodoo Herb and Root Magic* by catherine yronwode)

Tie a Dixie John root in a muslin bag and throw it in the washing machine with your bedding and night-clothes when you launder them. Make up the bed with this fixed bedding to increase your sexual stamina and encourage reciprocal energy from your partner.

LAUNDRY LIQUID FOR SPIRITUAL CLEANSING

To your regular laundry liquid, add 1 tablespoon of Chinese Wash, or 1/4 cup of water into which is dissolved a pinch each of Uncrossing and Run Devil Run bath crystals, or 1/4 cup of 13-Herb bath-tea. Mix well.

LAUNDRY WASH TO PROTECT FROM FOOT-TRACK MAGIC

During the rinse cycle, add a pinch each of Fear Not to Walk Over Evil and Fiery Wall of Protection bath crystals to a load of socks.

LAUNDRY WASH BEFORE A DATE

When washing the clothes you'll be wearing out on a date, add 1/2 cup of hot water into which you have dissolved a pinch each of Love Me, Kiss Me Now, and Bewitching bath crystals. Gay men and women can add Lavender Love Drops and/or Q bath crystals. Sex workers may add Cleo May and/or Jezebel bath crystals.

LAUNDRY WASH FOR SUCCESS IN TEST-TAKING

Tie Solomon Seal root slices and a pinch each of King Solomon Wisdom and Crown of Success bath crystals in a rag, and launder with your clothes.

FLOOR SPRINKLES

Floor sprinkles are herbs, mineral salts, or sachet powders that are cast onto the floor and remain there while a prayer is recited. Generally, they are swept or vacuumed up, but some sprinkles stay in place in the corners of a room or under rugs and mats. This is to sustain the work between wet washes. Floor sprinkles pre-date floor washes because in older times many homes had beaten earth floors rather than wood, stone, or tile, and washing an earthen floor would have left a muddy mess — but even today, there are certain times when you may prefer a dry floor sprinkle for speed of application and clean-up.

LEAH'S CLEANSING SWEEP AND CARPET SPRINKLE
Combine a package of Van Van sachet powder or bath crystals with a box of baking soda to cleanse and deodorize both floors and carpeting.

MOMMA STARR'S CLEANSING FLOOR SWEEP
Sprinkle coffee grounds from back to front of the room you're working in while praying. Let it sit for a little while. Sweep up. You can add a squeeze of lemon juice and/or a bit of baking soda if desired.

LUCKY GREEN RICE WITH CUT-UP MONEY FLOOR SWEEP
(from *Hoodoo Herb and Root Magic* by catherine yronwode)
Purchase Lucky Rice — raw rice dyed green which has been mixed with genuine cut-up dollar bills — and wear this prepared rice in your own shoes for 72 hours. Then scatter it about on the floor, sweep it up with a broom, and throw it out into your yard for prosperity, or in front of your business to bring in trade.

BASIL KITCHEN SWEEP FOR A HAPPY HOME
Sprinkle dried Basil on the kitchen floor, pray Psalms 23, and sweep everything out the back door, for "evil cannot stay where basil has been."

RUG SPRINKLE TO DRAW BUSINESS
(from *Hoodoo Herb and Root Magic* by catherine yronwode)
Sprinkle Irish Moss under the carpets in your place of business to hold a steady stream of paying customers.

In the late 19th century, the development of indoor plumbing systems led to the gradual replacement of portable sheet metal or wooden bathtubs with stationary enameled cast iron tub-and-shower combinations, such as this 1890s model. As outdoor bathing waned, the old hoodoo custom of "dumping the tub" to the East or to the West in a rite of magical disposal was replaced by reserving a symbolic cup of bath or shower water for later ritual deployment or disposal out of doors, in the yard, in the street, at a crossroads, or even at a cemetery.

HOW TO TAKE A SPIRITUAL BATH

Once you've decided the purpose of the spiritual bath you wish to take, you should decide whether it is to be a poured-over bath or a soaking bath. Prepare your bathing mixture accordingly. If you have sensitive skin or allergies you may dilute the tea with more water, as needed. There are a number of more or less elaborate ways to perform the bathing ritual but these twelve basic steps apply to most baths:

1. Start clean: Make sure that you're physically clean already. You do not need to take a pre-bath, but, for example, if you're going to be doing a pre-dawn spiritual bath, you should take a regular shower or bath with soap and water the night before, so that you wake up clean.

2. Bathe before dawn: Rise before Sun-up so that the bathing can be completed by the time the Sun rises. This is especially traditional if you are performing the spiritual bath for gain or increase of any kind, for as the Sun rises, so will good things come to you. However, if the bath you are taking is not to be taken before dawn, then respect the timing prescribed.

3. Add optional candles: If you're doing a cleansing, jinx removing, or uncrossing bath, you may wish to light a small tea light or white candle on either side of your tub or shower stall; even a small birthday candle will do if you're in a pinch. For other baths, a candle of appropriate colour anointed with suitable condition oil may be used if desired; however, you do not need a candle to take a spiritual bath.

4. Enter the bath: Take two or three long and deep breaths to calm your body and mind. If you have decided to use candles, then walk between them to enter the bathing area. If you are taking a pour-over bath, bring your pot of warm bath-tea diluted with water into the shower or tub with you. If you are taking a soaking bath, step into the tub of prepared water.

5. Pour or soak with prayers: If you are taking a poured bath in the shower or standing in a bath tub, pour the water over your head one cup at a time as you pray. If you are taking a soaking bath, immerse your body in the water. Either way, get your entire body wet and let the herbal essences seep into you as you pray from the Bible or from the heart. If your hairdo is such that you cannot wash your hair, bathe from the neck down and wash your face. If your hair permits, pour water over it or dunk your head under water to wet it.

6. Bathe with directionality: To rid yourself of a negative condition, such as a jinx, a streak of bad luck, an unnatural illness, or a bad habit that's been worrying you, wash downward, from head to toe. If you have filled the tub with water, you may start by soaking, then open the drain, stand up with your hands crossed, right hand on left shoulder and left hand on right shoulder, uncross your arms, and stroke downward with the palms of your hands. To bring in a desired result or circumstance, such as a faithful lover, a better job, higher wages, gambling luck, or more happiness in life, wash upward, from toe to head. If you are taking a pour-over bath, pour the water on yourself, then stroke upward, and finish by folding your hands in prayer.

7. Keep a representative sample of your bath water: This is the water with your essence in it. In the days before indoor plumbing, baths were taken out of doors and the entire tub was dumped out. Now, after a soaking bath, you may keep a cup by placing it in the tub and letting the water out the drain while it remains in place. If taking a pour-over bath, place a small bowl at your feet as you pour and let the container catch the liquid you'll keep.

8. Come out of your bath or shower and air dry: If you used candles at Step 3, exit the bath between them. You can drink a cup of your herb tea now (or another cup of herbal tea you've brewed) to enhance your spell as you air dry. It's also a great time to pray. Observe the changes you feel in your mind and body as the water evaporates from your skin.

9. After uncrossing, prepare for your blessings: If you've taken an uncrossing or cleansing bath, now is the time to oil or powder your body with a formula for luck, love, protection, or money.

10. Dress in clean clothes and dispose of the sample of water: Pour out the representative sample taken earlier either by casting it into your yard or into a crossroads. Throw the water East, toward the rising Sun, for gain, or toward the West, the direction of the setting Sun, for removal. No specific crossroad is required; choose one that is conveniently located for you. Walk or drive home and don't look back.

11. Use the left-over bath water in other rites: You may also keep some of your wash water to cleanse the home you live in or your place of business if you wish the work to extend to and affect these locations as well.

12. Stay clean as long as possible: Although it is rarely suggested nowadays, it is an old custom to try to avoid touching others or shaking their hands on the day that you have taken a spiritual bath. This is done to keep the work on you and to avoid getting messed up again.

BATHING BY PROXY

Ideally, any adult can perform a spiritual bath on his or her own and children are typically bathed by their parents. Sometimes however, it is necessary to give a spiritual bath to a person who is unwilling to take it, or is at a distance physically or, due to unfortunate circumstances, is incarcerated or hospitalized. In circumstances such as these, it is possible to perform the bath on an effigy or doll of the person, although most root workers will tell you that this practice is usually less successful than doing the work on the person themselves.

To begin with, a water-proof dolly or representation of the person needs to be made. A commercial plastic doll with a removable head, arms, and legs is a good choice. A figural candle or a beeswax figure is another alternative. If the doll is hollow, it can be filled with appropriate herbs, curios, or personal concerns from the target. If it is made of wax, the target's name should be inscribed into it, using a needle or the point of a knife.

Next the doll is baptized, to link it to the target person. There are a number of different ways to do this; what follows is a method recounted by catherine yronwode, the co-owner of the Lucky Mojo Curio Company and an accomplished reader and root doctor:

"I was taught how to do this many years ago in Oakland, California. The man who taught me called it "baptizing the dollie." He held the doll-baby in his left hand on its back, drew a cross over it in the air with his right index and middle finger (like a Christian blessing gesture), and then held his open, slightly cupped right hand, palm down, in the air over it, but not touching it, as he said:

[John Doe] you are, [downward stroke of cross on name]
And [John Doe] to me [cross-stroke of cross on name]
You will always be. [hand pauses over dollie for next part]
You will think what i tell you to think,
Walk where i tell you to walk,
Talk when i tell you to talk,
Do what i tell you to,
Go where i send you,
And speak when you're spoken to.
In Jesus' name, Amen.

"Another time when i asked this man to repeat the spell, he baptised the dollie with a different speech, spoken with more angry conviction:

[John Doe] you are, [downward stroke of cross on name]
And [John Doe] to me [cross-stroke of cross on name]
You will always be. [hand pauses over dollie for next part]
From this time henceforward,
You will go where i send you... [pause]
And i'm gon' send you to *Hell*
In Jesus' name, Amen.

"I came to understand that after the first three spoken lines with the drawing of the cross, he improvised or rapped the rest of the baptism depending upon the circumstances. There was no one set way he would say it, as there is among the German and British folks with their carefully memorized spoken rhymes. I have adapted his form and i use it with success, modifying it on the spot as the need arises, to baptise both love-dolls and destruction dolls."

At this point the doll is ready to handle. Treat it as you would the target; bathe it as a person would be bathed. The making, timing, and disposal of a doll's bath is unchanged from the recipes given, except that less volume is required; the bath is simply given to the doll as a representative of the target.

Bathing a doll is also a way to work sneaky, hidden tricks when the purpose is to coerce or harm someone. Crossing baths are seldom used on living people, but working by proxy, you can successfully bathe a target in formulas intended for destruction.

A doll such as this may be used not only for bathing but in other spells or tricks. For instance, fixed and prepared candles may be burned around the doll, it can smoked with incense, dressed in special clothing, and, if called by name, it may be influenced by your words, songs, commands, or prayers.

When the work is completed you can keep the doll for future use. If it was made for healing, it can be given to the person it represents for safe-keeping. Should the doll no longer be required, you can call the person's spirit out of the doll prior to disposal. The personal concerns from the doll can be cleaned off and kept for re-use or disposed of, as you see fit.

Read more on working with doll babies online at
Forum.LuckyMojo.com//doll-baby,-voodoo-doll,-poppet-questions-and-answers-t8946.html

TIMING WHEN TO BATHE

There are many "ideal" times for different baths — however the point is to do the work when you need it. Waiting a week to do an Uncrossing bath when you are crossed up and suffering right now just makes no sense!

WORKING BY THE HANDS OF THE CLOCK
As the clock hands fall, cast spells like Uncrossing or Block-Buster, to take evil away. As the hands rise, work to draw in love, money, and luck.

For example: To take off a trick that has blocked your rise in business and to draw in steady work, prepare a Jinx Killer bath at 9:05 in the morning, a typical hour to start work for the day, but as the minute hand is falling. Enter the bath around 9:20 and stay there until 9:29. Let the water go down the drain, and the bad energy will go with it. Air-dry and dress your feet and head with Crown of Success and Steady work oils. By now it will be about 9:45 and both the clock hands will be rising, bringing in good fortune.

WORKING BY THE DAYS OF THE WEEK
If there is time to wait and your situation is not urgent, then it is possible to combine working by the hours of the clock with a day of the week that is helpfully aligned to your situation.

- **Monday:** The Moon's day. Good for works of psychic vision, marital fidelity, femininity, fertility, and caring for children.
- **Tuesday:** Mars' day. Used to conquer a situation or a person, for aggression and virility, for robust good health, and for strength.
- **Wednesday:** Mercury's day. Suitable for works of safe travel, speech, written communication, negotiation, gambling, and speed.
- **Thursday:** Jupiter's day. A good choice for money and job related works, and for success in business, legal, and worldly affairs.
- **Friday:** Venus' day. Has a positive influence on love work, petitions for luxury and wealth, and when one desires admiration and beauty.
- **Saturday:** Saturn's day. A day for revenge, justice work, divine retribution, binding foes, and crossing up enemies.
- **Sunday:** The Sun's day. Chosen for its optimistic and successful energy, to accomplish positive works, and to engender good health.

Going back to the previous example, you would clear away messes on a Sunday and improve job prospects on a Thursday.

WORKING BY THE PHASES OF MOON

Works of increase are done during a waxing or growing Moon, whereas works of decrease or removal are done during a waning or wasting Moon. In hoodoo, the astronomical New Moon is called the dark of the Moon, and we use the first visible crescent, called the change of the Moon, as the time that traditionally marks the start of the waxing phase.

Returning to the example we've been using; Start Jinx Breaking on your money during the waning Moon to take off tricks against your finances. Then during the waxing Moon, switch to Steady Work and Money Drawing baths with a petition to draw regular employment and a good salary.

WORKING BY THE SIGNS OF MOON

Every month the Moon rushes rapidly through the signs of the zodiac, spending about 2 1/2 days in each sign. You will need a Farmer's Almanac or a Moon calendar to catch the signs, but once you do, you can take advantage of their natural energies.

Using our previous example, Pisces, the last sign of the zodiac, removes influences, while Virgo is for office jobs. A Jinx Killer bath with the Moon in Pisces and a Steady Work bath with the Moon in Virgo would be ideal.

COMBINING TIMINGS

You can combine two or more timings. For instance, you could bathe to remove the employment jinx as the clock hands fall, on Sunday, during a waning Moon in Pisces, then bathe for a better job as the clock hands rise, on Thursday, during a waxing Moon in Virgo. The more timing factors you incorporate in your work, the better: but any of these methods works well alone. Do the work when you need it and choose the best timing you can.

Read more about working by the hours of the clock online at
Forum.LuckyMojo.com//spell-timing-time-of-day-or-night,-clock-time-t11842.html

Read more about working by the days of the week online at
Forum.LuckyMojo.com/spell-timing-planetary-influences-days-of-the-week-t1429.html

Read more about working with the phases and signs of the Moon at
Forum.LuckyMojo.com/spell-timing-moon-phases,-moon-signs,-moon-void-of-course-t442.html
LuckyMojo.com/moonphases.html

PRAYERS FOR THE BATH

Although hoodoo is a set of culturally shared magical practices and not a religion, its development has been inextricably informed by and linked to Christianity and, to a lesser extent, to Judaism's influence on Christianity. The bodily preparation for the bath, reasons for bathing, and the waters used in conjure bear many of the same attributes that can be found in Jewish bathing practices. Jewish mikvahs or "pools" for ritual cleansing are rooted in the spiritual. The chest-deep natural waters, usually obtained from rainfall or melted snow, are used in conjunction with prayer to cleanse the body and soul from defilement; to prepare for a life transition such as marriage; to mark the end the menstrual cycle of a married woman and ready her for renewed marital intimacy; to move to a higher level of spiritual involvement; to prepare the body for burial, and to facilitate the conversion of a gentile to the Jewish religion. The body must be scrupulously clean prior to entry in the mikvah and immersion must be total, down to the very last hair.

Parallels between Jewish bathing rites, Christian baptism, and spiritual bathing in the hoodoo tradition are evident, from the preference for natural waters to the cleaning of the body prior to entering the water. All three systems make use of water to clean the body while the rites mark important moments and passages in an individual's life. All three are living traditions.

Although people of any religion can practice hoodoo should they so choose, most African American practitioners have grown up in Protestant Christian families, with a particularly large representation from the Baptist denomination. As a result, Baptist traditions of gesture and spoken cadence subtly shape and contextualise much of the prayer used in conjure.

Prayers are said while the bathing mixture is prepared, used, and disposed of. Some are general requests asking for God's help or dedicating the work in the name of the Father, the Son, and the Holy Ghost. Others are verses of scripture, particularly the Psalms, which either have long associations to acts of magic, or were chosen due to their applicability to a given situation. The common thread of all these prayers is their provenance: the Bible.

Like all religious texts, the Bible is a Book of Power. It has passages which address pretty much any situation that can arise in a person's life and it contains words of wisdom that remain true without respect to creed or denomination. This wealth of advice is available to all, even if a bit of humility is necessary for some people to make use of it.

To locate appropriate portions of scripture for your bath, read the Bible, refer to books on the topic, or search online sites which collect passages by purpose. Read through various verses and chapters before selecting one for your bath. Listen to your intuition and allow yourself to be Spirit-led. Here are some selections from the Bible for different conditions:
• **Uncrossing:** Romans 12:21; 2 Timothy 4:18; Matthew 6:13.
• **Protection:** Isaiah 41:10; Isaiah 54:17.
• **Love:** The Song of Solomon has many excellent selections.
• **Financial Success:** Proverbs 10:22; Proverbs 11:24-25.
• **Psychic Vision:** Romans 12:6; 1 Corinthians 12:10; 1 Timothy 4:14.
• **Blessings and Fertility:** Genesis 1:28; Genesis 9:1; Genesis 9:7.
• **To Heal Marital Strife:** Colossians 3:19; Matthew 6:14-15.
• **For Child Support:** 1 Timothy 5:8; Romans 12:19; Zechariah 11:17.

Psalms are the prayers most commonly chosen to accompany spiritual baths. Their popularity in hoodoo came about through the publication of the old Jewish magical book "Secrets of the Psalms," which has been available via mail-order since the late 1800s. An entire Psalm, or a portion of it, may be recited once, or a prescribed number of times, while bathing and there are traditional Psalms to say for almost every condition one could imagine.

These are some of the most popular Psalms in rootwork:
• **Psalm 23:** General blessings, luck, wisdom and prosperity.
• **Psalm 37:** Protection from enemies and back-biting.
• **Psalm 46:** To soothe fighting within a couple and end marital strife.
• **Psalm 51:** Forgiveness from sin, particularly after crossing work.
• **Psalm 61:** To bless a home; to find shelter.
• **Psalm 65:** Road-opening work which breaks through barriers.
• **Psalm 91:** Protection from danger and distress; keep evil spirits away.

Another way to choose a passage is by bibliomancy or book-divination. State your situation while holding a Bible in your hands. Randomly open it to a page and let your finger move about the page until you feel it can stop. Look at the chapter and verse pointed to by your finger. Alternatively, let your eyes pick out the first passage they see and read the passage through.

The complete Book of Psalms, with magical prescriptions, is online at **ReadersAndRootworkers.org/wiki/Category:The_Book_of_Psalms** Read more about the Psalms and other Biblical prayers in these books:
"Secrets of the Psalms" by Godfrey Selig
"Hoodoo Bible Magic" by Miss Michaele and Prof. Charles Porterfield

DRINKING TEAS AND BATHING

In past centuries, when medical care was less easily obtained than it is today, the local root doctor was often the local herbalist as well as the magical practitioner. It was then common for a conjure doctor's client to be given salves, poultices, and teas in conjunction with prescribed spiritual baths. These herb-based prescriptions eased physical symptoms while, at the same time, spiritual issues were being addressed with spell work.

The knowledge of local North American herbs and their use in treating both physical illness and spiritual conditions was passed along to the black community via the Native American tribes, most notably the Cherokee. The use of Pine in hoodoo as both a cleanser of negativity and as a remedy for bronchial conditions and rheumatism is a classic example of this.

It was customary at that time for both herbalists and conjure doctors to make use of highly purgative or emetic herbs as drinking teas, particularly during uncrossing work, the belief being that the system would empty itself of the illness or jinx. Given that food poisoning was one of the main causes of illness at the time, this choice of herbs seems quite logical.

Non-purgative herbs that have historically been used in hoodoo as beverages, as well as in baths or washes, include Celery seed or Dandelion root tea to increase psychic vision, Chamomile Tea for money-luck, and Life Everlasting tea taken on a weekly basis to promote longevity.

Over the years, as herbal medicine has fallen out of use, the practice of drinking magical herbal teas, as well as that of using herb-based salves and liniments, has faded and all but disappeared from modern rootwork. It is a practice well worth reviving, however, as it can be both soothing to the soul and supportive to your spiritual work to drink a cup of properly selected herbal tea during bathing or between baths. Ingesting a spiritual beverage allows the selected herbal ingredients to act both internally and externally. You are bathing all parts of yourself.

When choosing a tea, it is wise to stay away from herbs with very strong purgative, cathartic, or emetic action since they can be quite hard on the system unless used under the direction of a skilled medical herbalist. Herbs to avoid drinking include Bitter Aloes, Blue Flag, High John the Conqueror, Senna, Cascara Sagrada, and Lobelia, amongst others. Happily, many safer choices of spiritual herbs are available for use in tea that have a pleasant flavor and no dangerous side-effects.

In general, you can make herbal teas for internal use by using 1/2 to 1 teaspoon of loose dried or fresh herb per cup of water. Infuse leafy herbs and blossoms, decoct hard roots or berries, then skim, strain, or decant the beverage and sweeten to taste. Instructions for these procedures can be found on page 12 of this book. If your tea is too strong, dilute it with hot water. Herbal teas that are safe for internal use and appropriate for various commonly-encountered spiritual conditions include:

- **Ancestor Work:** Althaea Leaf Tea
- **Controlling:** Licorice Root Tea
- **Courage:** Yarrow Blossom Tea
- **Court Cases:** Sumac Tea or Little John (Galangal) Tea
- **Fidelity:** Red Clover Top Tea or Raspberry Leaf Tea
- **Friendship:** Clove Tea
- **Gambling:** Chamomile Tea
- **Happy Home:** Basil Tea or Lavender Tea
- **Health:** Sarsaparilla Root or Self-Heal Leaf Tea
- **Law Keep Away:** Fennel Seed Tea or Oregano Tea
- **Love:** Rose Petal Tea
- **Love Uncrossing:** Dill Leaf Tea
- **Luck:** Cinnamon Tea
- **Lust and Sexuality:** Cubeb Berry Tea
- **Money:** Chamomile Tea
- **Necromancy:** Mullein Leaf Tea
- **Protection:** Mint Tea
- **Psychic Vision:** Dandelion Root Tea or Jasmine Tea
- **Road Opening:** Lemongrass Tea
- **Sleep and Sweet Dreams:** Hops Tea
- **Uncrossing:** Nettle Leaf Tea or Coffee

The purchase of a few basic medical and magical herbal guides is a good investment if you intend to work with herbs or formulate herbal mixtures for internal use or local external application.

Read more about working with and preparing herbs in these books:

"The Way of Herbs" by Michael Tierra
"The Herbal Medicine Maker's Handbook" by James Green
"Prescription for Herbal Healing" by Phyllis A. Balch
"Hoodoo Herb and Root Magic" by catherine yronwode
"Encyclopedia of Magical Herbs" by Scott Cunningham

BATHING BODY PARTS

In the modern era, when indoor plumbing and hot water heaters are the norm, bathing is usually considered to be a whole-body affair. However, in the past, when water was at a premium and every pot of it had to be heated over a fire, it was quite common for practitioners to wash certain portions or parts of the body in a stand-alone manner. Even with the introduction of modern conveniences, this older way of working is preserved in hoodoo, especially under specific circumstances,

Body parts are washed prior to certain activities, such as gambling, hairdressing, contact sports, or playing music, or for specific purposes, like uncrossing, protection, spiritual blessing, or easing physical pain. They are typically prepared with bath crystals, herbs, soaps, or oils. Additionally, the water with which they are made may be enhanced with a splash of Florida Water, Holy Water, or Hoyt's Cologne, according to the purpose of the work.

• **Hands:** The hands my be cleansed with a special wash or perfume in preparation for activities that require luck or manual dexterity, such as gambling, typing, cosmetology, or playing music. The hands and arms may also be cleansed up to the elbows after one has performed negative work, such as jinxing enemies or lighting black candles on their names.

• **Feet:** Biblical precedent for this ritual goes back to the day when Jesus washed his disciples' feet, cited in John 13:1-15. Traditionally, foot washing is not done for oneself, but is performed on a client by a root doctor for the purposes of blessing, healing, or taking off crossed conditions, and it is accompanied by prayers. Foot baths are also medically useful for people who have reduced mobility or suffer from diabetes or arthritic conditions. The foot washing may be followed by a light oiling of the feet to bring in luck, protection, health, or blessings.

• **Limbs:** A warm wash and rub of the limbs is helpful when there is pain in the arms or legs, such as with arthritis and rheumatism. A salt scrub or a bath-tea made with counter-irritant herbs will stimulate circulation. One typical remedy to cure pain or conjuration in the limbs is to rub freely with a tea or bath of Red Pepper, salt, and silver money.

• **Head:** Head, face, and neck baths are used in hoodoo when there is confusion of mind or headache. A cool wash is good to soften and calm down someone who is hot-headed or angry. The head may then be lightly dressed with a condition oil for success, wisdom, clarity, or luck.

DISSOLVING WORDS IN WATER

As a bathing mixture is prepared, it is prayed over. Typically, a portion of scripture or a Psalm is recited along with a petition-prayer. Another method of conveying scriptural power to the water involves dissolving Bible verses, prayers, or petitions in the bath water. This practice comes to hoodoo from the contributing influences of Middle Eastern, African, and European magic.

The earliest records that describe the dissolving of written words in liquids for magical purposes date back to antiquity. The practice has been attributed to the ancient Egyptians, Greeks, and Romans. Typically, the spell would be written out and then the paper would be soaked in wine or water, causing the ink to dissolve into the fluid. The liquid would then be drunk, releasing the spell into the body, which would then acquire its power.

In Africa, prayers may be soaked in liquids and drunk, but additionally, the worker might burn the paper to ash and mix the ash into water. This way of working with ash is not used as often as other methods in modern hoodoo, but it is nonetheless a useful addition to one's repertoire.

In Jewish folk magic, there are countless variations on the theme of ingesting and bathing in prayers. These include spells written, dissolved and drunk as above; as well as prayers and inscriptions made on food and then consumed. Speaking a prayer over prepared liquids or foods at the table is another Jewish custom, one that formed the foundation for the Christian practice known as "saying Grace."

The marking of bread dough with religious symbols that are then folded or symbolically dissolved back into the dough as it is kneaded is a feature of Swedish trolldom folk magic as well.

It is thought that these early dissolved spells gave birth to the later love philters and potions of Medieval magic which require being swallowed for efficacy. The transmission of the effects of the brew to the body via consumption was informed by ancient practices, although later on individual ingredients came to be of greater importance than the written word.

Practically speaking, with regards to spiritual bathing practices in hoodoo, the dissolving of words in water can be particularly useful when a cup of herbal bath-tea will be drunk by the bather. Working in this manner is also a way of transmitting a petition, prayer, or command to a target individual without their knowledge. In any case, make sure to use a non-toxic ink or fruit juice to write the words which will be dissolved.

DEPLOYMENT AND DISPOSAL OF WATERS

Deployment uses a physical item — in this case scrub or bath water — to trick or fix a person, place, or thing. The target comes into contact with it.

- **Floor Wash:** Floor scrubs are deployed to draw better business, good clientele, money, luck, or love. You can mix remnant bath water into mop water to wash the home, porch, sidewalk, or place of business.
- **Shampoo or Body Wash:** Mix a small amount of bath water into your target's shampoo or body wash for love or domination work. This is also done, albeit less commonly, with diluted baths such as Cast Off Evil, Fear Not to Walk Over Evil, Uncrossing, and Protection.
- **Laundry:** Mix about a cup of bath water into a full load of laundry. This is particularly effective for socks, underwear, and bed linens; the uses are the same as for shampoo or body wash given above.
- **Cooking:** Unsoaped bath water from Love Me, Influence, and I Can You Can't type baths can be included in small amounts in the cooking of meals or baking of food to be eaten by the target of the work.
- **Footsteps or Foot-Tracks:** Mop water or bath water can be thrown into a path to affect someone who steps on it or to influence a person's comings or goings; this is used with both love spells and crossing spells.

Disposal is the process of getting rid of remnant water at a special location. The target need not contact it; disposal itself sets the work in motion.

- **Sunrise / East:** To draw luck or to make something grow or prosper.
- **Sunset / West:** To remove evil or to make something wane or sicken.
- **Front Yard:** To draw something or someone in, to attract luck, money, or love; to provide protection against spiritual invasion.
- **Back Yard:** To keep something or someone close, to hold it down or to keep it as it is; for instance, to keep a lover or spouse at home.
- **Tree:** Used to absorb negative energy; a strong, old tree is best.
- **Crossroads:** This is an all-purpose disposal site for spells; a place to seal, finish, or fix a trick and to disperse positive or negative energies into the world. A common adjuration is to "toss your left-over bath water over your shoulder into a crossroads and don't look back."
- **Graveyard:** To end or kill something; not often used with bath water.

INGREDIENTS FOR TEAS, BATHS, AND WASHES

Floor washes, baths, and teas consist of water in which is dissolved or suspended a variety of minerals, liquids, oils, herb-teas, and spiritual soaps. Let's take a look at the most popular and commonly-encountered of these.

SPECIAL WATERS

Hoodoo retains a tradition of choosing special waters for their magical qualities. If difficult to obtain, they may be extended by adding tap water.

- **Spring Water:** Natural moving water that emerges from the earth is good for pretty much any situation; it has a lively, uplifting energy.
- **Rain Water:** Natural water fallen from the sky; it should be used as fresh as possible, especially for blessing and cleansing baths.
- **Storm Water:** Water that falls from the sky when there is lightning and thunder can cause fights and discord; it has a heavy, aggressive energy.
- **Snow Water:** Natural water fallen from the sky in frozen form, melted to form a liquid; it is quieting, tranquil, soothing and meditative; it will take a very large quantity of snow to make enough water for a full bath.
- **River Water:** Natural moving water, soothing and renewing to the soul; it takes away troubles and moves unwanted things or people away.
- **Lake Water:** Natural water from a confined body of water; it ranges from stabilizing to stagnating, depending on the source.
- **Ocean Water:** Natural water from the seas is used in spells for travel or to induce movement in things or people. If caught on the ebbing tide, it removes influences; if caught on the rising tide, it brings influences in.
- **Stump Water:** Stagnant water accumulated in the rotting stump of a tree; it is used for crossing, to cause sickness, and to remove warts.
- **Holy Water:** Water blessed by a pastor or priest; it is added to baths for healing, uncrossing, blessing, and protection against evil.
- **Tears:** Water generated by the body in a physical response to joy, sadness, anger, or other extreme emotional state; it is used to infuse a specific state of mind or emotional intent; it is also a personal concern.
- **Water of Seven Waters:** A special healing blend made from seven positive types of water or from water gathered at seven sacred locations; it is added to baths intended to support physical healing from disease.

LIQUIDS OTHER THAN WATER

Liquids other than water included in a bath may be aromatic, sour, sweet, or bitter in nature. The amount used depends on their toxicity or strength.

- **Ammonia:** Used in very small quantities, this household cleaner is employed to strip away crossed conditions and turn things around.
- **Coffee:** A powerful stimulant, it also strips away crossed conditions and negative energy; one strong cup is the usual amount in a bath.
- **Vinegar:** Apple-cider vinegar, red wine vinegar, and pickling vinegar are protective and also can be used to "sour" a situation.
- **Turpentine:** The Cherokee of Georgia favoured pine for cleansing, but their descendants often use turpentine to remove evil airs, influences, and energies. It is a strong solvent; only a few drops are needed.
- **Tar Water:** Originally made with pine tar, now often made with petroleum tar, it is traditionally used in uncrossing, but overexposure is toxic and if improperly disposed of it pollutes the soil and waterways.
- **Pine-Sol:** This popular commercial cleaning product safely conveys the piney goodness of Native cleansing traditions to the modern home.
- **Urine:** Used to wash down walk-ways for business success or protection.
- **Sexual Fluids:** Used in baths for love, sexual influence, or domination.
- **Honey or Syrup:** For sweetness, love, glamour, and romance.
- **Colognes and Toilet Waters:** Hoyt's Cologne, Florida Water, Orange Cologne, and Rose Cologne bring luck, cleansing, marriage, and love.
- **Herbal Distillates or Hydrosols:** Rose Water, Orange Water, and Willow Water are used in cooking and to scent bath waters as well.
- **Milk:** Used in beauty baths, it is also soothing and nurturing.
- **Dressing Oils and Essential Oils:** Condition oils and scented oils are used for specific spiritual effects as well as for aromatic purposes.
- **Chinese Wash:** This traditional floor wash also makes a good cleansing addition to the bath and works well to fix laundry.

MOMMA STARR'S UNCROSSING BATH
Combine 1 cup black coffee, 1 capful of ammonia, and 1/2 cup salt.

MISS CAT'S SPIRITUAL WORKER'S HEALING BATH
Mix 1/2 cup vinegar, 1 quart White Oak tea, and 1/2 cup Epsom salts.

MINERALS

Mineral baths are some of the most traditional conjure baths. The number of ingredients in a mineral bath mix can vary. Some practitioners favour an odd number of ingredients; others do not count. Many of the old 3-ingredient baths include 1, 2, or 3 minerals, with or without added liquids or herbs. Below is a list of the minerals most common in bathing mixtures:

- **Salt:** Sodium chloride, sea salt, mineral salt, rock salt, pickling salt, kosher salt, and table salt; used for purification and protection.
- **Epsom Salt:** Magnesium sulfate; a mild laxative; it is used to remove unwanted conditions and it also makes a skin-soothing bath.
- **Bath Salts or Bath Crystals:** A pre-mixed combination of salt and Epsom salt; borax (sodium borate) and dried herbs may also be added.
- **Baking Soda or Washing Soda:** Washing soda is more common in the laundry and baking soda is more popular in cooking and as a deodorant.
- **Blueing:** Laundry blueing such as Reckitt's Squares, anil blueing balls, or Mrs. Stewart's (but not toxic blue vitriol or copperas) are used to whiten laundry and, in baths, to soothe the spirit.
- **Ash:** Usually a burnt petition, name, or prayer; added to a bath it empowers what it is added to with the essence of its power.
- **Red Brick Dust:** Protective; it helps keep enemies and the law away.
- **Saltpeter or Gunpowder:** Ignites the work, gives it a bang.
- **Sulphur:** For crossing, but also sometimes used to harshly purify.
- **Sugar:** Technically, this is a crystalline solid rather than a mineral since it comes from plants; it is used in baths for luck and love.

MISS CAT'S SPIRITUAL CLEANSING MINERAL BATH #1
Combine 1/2 cup salt, 1/2 cup Epsom salt, and 1 tablespoon saltpeter.

MINERAL BATH FOR SUCCESS IN BUSINESS
Dissolve 1/2 square of blueing with 1 tablespoon each saltpeter and sugar.

DEACON MILLETT'S PROTECTION SCRUB
Mix 1 tablespoon each kosher salt, Epsom salt, and sugar, plus 3 finely crumbled Bay leaves. Rub this briskly on your skin, then rinse in plenty of clear water. Alternatively, this blend may be used for a soaking bath.

HERBS

Herbal bath-teas not only have a spiritual use, but have also been used therapeutically for centuries. The skin is the largest organ of assimilation and elimination of the body and thus the medicinal and spiritual effects of herbs and minerals are readily absorbed through the pores.

Older hoodoo herbal bath recipes tend to carry an African emphasis on substances that are hot or spicy, like Cinnamon, Mustard, and Cayenne. Others, such as Hyssop, are mentioned in the Bible. Native American herbs were added by direct cultural contact. A wider array of botanicals, reflecting both European and Native influences, entered hoodoo during the late 19th century via the grimoires and packaged herbs carried by the order houses.

Either fresh or dried herbs are suitable for use in bathing. You may need a larger quantity of fresh than dried, because they are watery.

As with the mineral baths, some workers prefer to use an odd number of ingredients in their blends, while others do not count out their ingredients.

- **Agrimony:** To reverse a jinx, curse, or hex.
- **Allspice:** For luck, prosperity, and business success.
- **Borage:** Added to Peace Water to make a peaceful home floor wash.
- **Broom Straws:** To uncross, cleanse, and protect the home.
- **Chamomile:** For gambling luck; good for hand washes.
- **Cinnamon:** For money drawing and luck in gambling or business.
- **Cubebs:** For sexual passion; sprinkle the used berries around the yard.
- **Eucalyptus:** To cast off evil and remove bad influences.
- **Hyssop:** To remove sin and crossed conditions.
- **Lemongrass:** To cleanse and also to turn bad luck to good.
- **Mint:** For cleansing, protection, and to reverse jinxes.
- **Oak Bark:** For good health and spiritual cleansing.
- **Pine Needles:** To remove negativity and also to draw money.
- **Raspberry Leaves:** Used by women for marital fidelity.
- **Red Pepper:** For protection and cleansing.
- **Rose Petals:** For love, romance, and sexual pleasure.
- **Rue:** To remove the evil eye and protect from envy.
- **Sassafras Root Bark:** To increase wealth and make money last.
- **Wahoo Bark:** To take off crossed conditions and break jinxes.
- **Walnuts (Black):** To fall out of love.
- **White Mustard:** To uncross and protect.

HOW TO MAKE AND STORE HERB BATHS BY THE BATCH

If baths are to be taken for a number of days in a row, then rather than brewing new tea every day, just make up to a three days' supply at a time, strain it, and keep in the refrigerator. Herb tea doesn't keep indefinitely, though, so larger batches should be frozen in individual containers. When needed, these "bath-cubes" are easy to reheat in a saucepan or microwave.

WOMAN'S MARITAL FELICITY AND FIDELITY HERB BATH

Regularly take baths in a strong tea of Raspberry leaves or use the tea as a wash for the genitals to keep a man from straying.

HERB BATH TO OVERCOME SHYNESS

Make a strong decoction of John the Conqueror root chips, Ginseng root chips, Master root chips, and Lovage root slices, simmering the roots at low heat for 21 minutes in a quart of water. Strain it and boil off the liquid to reduce and concentrate the total contents to a pint or so. Add the concentrate to a basin or large pot of hot water. Add dried Deer's Tongue leaf and infuse it for another 9 minutes. Strain again and dilute in a full tub of bath water. Pray Psalms 23 as you bathe, and dispose of the water at sunrise, at a crossroads. Take this bath once a week for nine weeks.

HERB BATH TO UNTIE A WOMAN'S NATURE

You will need 3 parts Nettle, 1 part Sarsaparilla root, 1 part Hyssop, 1 part Angelica root, and 1/2 part Sage. Boil the Angelica and Sarsaparilla while envisioning yourself as the sensual strong woman who loves sex as you did before being tied. Read from the Song of Solomon if you wish. Once the roots have simmered for 15 minutes, turn off the heat and add the Nettle, Hyssop, and Sage to break the negative work that's been done on you. Steep for half an hour. Add the herb tea to your bath and keep aside a cup to dilute and drink internally. It won't taste great, but it does the job and it's non-toxic. However, do not consume it if you're pregnant, as both Angelica and Hyssop are contraindicated in pregnancy.

Read more about herbs and their spiritual uses online at
Herb-Magic.com
Read hundreds of recipes for the use of herbs in magic in this book:
"Hoodoo Herb and Root Magic" by catherine yronwode

OILS

One of the most economical ways to prepare a quick spiritual bath is to float a few drops of oil on the water. You may use one or more condition oils from a spiritual supply house, selecting and blending the formulas you want according to your situation. Popular condition oils for use in the bath include:

• **Healing Oil:** A soothing oil for those dealing with illness or pain.
• **Love Me Oil:** The most popular of the love oils; it has a floral scent.
• **Money Drawing Oil:** The leader in financial magic; its aroma is spicy.
• **7-11 Holy Oil:** A variation on the sacred Jewish Holy Oil of the Bible.
• **Special Oil No. 20:** Blended to bring in love, luck, health, and wealth.

Condition oil formulas are combined scents. Depending on the inclination of the maker, they may contain essential oils (distilled from plants), fragrance oils (artificial "laboratory" scents) and/or synthetic scents (compounds that mimic natural scents and may contain essential and/or artificial fragrances).

Some practitioners want to blend their own compounds or use "single note" scents, like Rosemary, Orange, or Musk, but they worry about working with uncut essentials, because so many of them are irritating to the skin.

To avoid guesswork, simply purchase "skin-safe" oils — single note oils properly blended into neutral carrier oils. Use them singly or mix them to create your own bath oil blends. If you let the mixture "work" together for at least one week, it will improve; a full month will bring out the best fragrance.

Here are three quick and easy skin-safe oil recipes from Leah Rivera:

LEAH'S QUICK AND EASY SPIRITUAL CLEANSING OIL
Mix equal parts Lucky Mojo Skin-Safe Lemongrass Oil, Hyssop Oil, and Camphor Oil. Add a pinch each of dried Lemongrass and Hyssop leaves.

LEAH'S QUICK AND EASY LOVING OIL
Mix equal parts Lucky Mojo Skin-Safe Rose Oil, Rose Geranium Oil, and Musk Oil. Add a pinch each of dried Rose petals and Lovage root chips.

LEAH'S QUICK AND EASY MONEY AND BUSINESS OIL
Mix equal parts Lucky Mojo Skin-Safe Cinnamon Oil, Bayberry Oil, and Mint Oil. Add a pinch each of Cinnamon chips, Mint, and crushed pyrite.

SPIRITUAL SOAPS

Spiritual soaps can carry your work on between baths. Some commercial soaps have a long history of use for spiritual conditions and soaps scented with single note oils are also employed in magic, according to the meanings associated with their botanical scents. Say a prayer before deploying soap in an area where others will use it, or pray while using the product yourself.

- **African Black Soap:** To reverse evil, to cleanse, to honour ancestors.
- **Bee and Flower Rose Soap:** For love, romance, and pleasure.
- **Black and White Soap:** For cross-cultural love and marriage.
- **Black Pullet Egg Soap:** For uncrossing; to take off jinxes.
- **Eucalyptus Soap:** To send away evil people and eliminate bad habits.
- **Fan Medicated Soap:** For uncrossing; to get rid of spirits and ghosts.
- **Florida Water Soap:** For cleansing, purification, and refreshment.
- **Lavender Soap:** For friendship and true love; also for gay love.
- **Parrot Green Soap:** For money drawing and business luck.
- **Octagon Soap:** To draw good luck and remove crossed conditions.
- **Rosemary Soap:** For a loving, peaceful home.
- **Lemon Soap:** To cut and clear away unwanted influences or people.
- **Lemongrass Soap:** For uncrossing and then drawing in good luck.
- **Mint Soap:** For mental clarity and personal protection.
- **Mysore Sandal Soap:** Scented with Sandalwood; for house blessings.
- **Patchouli Soap:** For good luck in love and money.
- **Rose Soap:** For romance, love, and sexuality.

AFRICAN BLACK SOAP TO REMOVE A MESS
Write the name of a person or a condition that is bothering you 4 times on paper. Rub African Black Soap on the name, thinking of the mess being out of your life. When you can no longer see the name, fold the paper away from your heart, and put it under a rock far from where you live.

A LOVE DOLL CARVED FROM SOAP
Carve a love-doll from Patchouli or Rose scented soap, name it for your lover and talk to it every time you bathe, rubbing it on your body, and telling it how much you want love. As the doll shrinks over days of use, tell your lover that his resistance is melting and that he must come to you.

RECIPES FOR SPIRITUAL BATHS AND WASHES

Use the following scratch-made recipes and spiritual supply blends to concoct floor washes and bath-teas for various conditions and situations.

BATHS FOR UNCROSSING

These baths rid you of crossed-up conditions, take off the evil eye, undo curses, reverse bad luck, or break a jinx. They can also remove the weight of a miserable day or the negativity of those around you.

- **Cast Off Evil Bath Crystals:** To get rid of bad habits and bad people.
- **Jinx Killer Bath Crystals:** To destroy or take away a jinx.
- **Reversing Bath Crystals:** To send a curse back to the sender.
- **Uncrossing Bath Crystals:** To remove crossed conditions.
- **Van Van Bath Crystals:** To change bad luck to good.
- **13-Herb Bath:** An herb mix used just like Uncrossing Bath Crystals.

SIMPLE BATH TO TAKE OFF CROSSED CONDITIONS
1 cup sea salt, 1 cup Epsom salt, 1 cup Apple cider vinegar.

JINX-REVERSING BATH
Make a decoction with a handful of Eucalyptus leaves. Strain and mix in 1/2 cup bath salts and 9 drops of Reversing Oil.

STRONG MESS REMOVAL BATH
Mix 1/4 teaspoon Chinese Wash, 1 cup strong coffee, 1 cup kosher salt; this is enough for a full soaking bath.

FORGIVENESS FROM SIN BATH
After performing crossing or cursing work, bathe in a strong tea of Hyssop while praying Psalms 51. Reserve a cup of weak Hyssop tea to drink (unless you are pregnant, in which case forego the tea).

JINX-KILLER FOOT BATH
Add 1 teaspoon ground Black Pepper to a packet of Jinx Killer Bath Crystals. Use in foot baths to take off tricks you may have stepped over.

BATH AND TEA TO REMOVE TRICKS LAID IN FOOD

If you feel that you have been tricked through something put into your food, you will want to be able to bathe externally and also to drink an uncrossing tea. Get a silver dime; it must have been made before 1965, for from that year onward, dimes were not made of silver. File all of the ridges off of the dime and save them in a little bottle of water. Bury the now-ridgeless dime in your yard. When you need to uncross yourself, make a cup of strong and hot Nettle leaf tea, remove it from the heat, and strain out the herbs. Add a quart of milk to the strained liquid, and then pour in the silver dime filings. Let this sit for half an hour. Carefully decant the milky liquid, leaving the silver dime filings in the bottom of your pot. Gently heat the liquid. Reserve one cup to drink and bathe with the rest. After your bath, wash the saved silver dime filings with fresh water and return them to their little bottle. They may be used this way again and again, until you feel that their power is all used up. Then you can bury them where you buried the dime.

BLUE BATH TO REMOVE NEGATIVE ENERGY

This bath is for taking off crossed conditions caused by exposure to natural negative energy, such having been in a disaster or falling into a deep feeling of sadness. Dissolve a square of Reckitts' Crown Blue or a Blue Anil Ball in a pot of very hot water. Add 1 teaspoon of Lemon juice and a few drops of Van Van Oil. Dilute this into a bathtub of warm water for bathing. If you wish, you may also use it for washing off any object that you feel has been touched by a negative person, including any amulets, crystals, or talismans of yours that have lost their energy.

UNCROSSING WITH BROOM STRAWS

A bath-tea made with Broom Corn straws is great for removing crossed conditions; just as a broom sweeps away bad things, so does a Broom Corn straw bath. If you do not have Broom Corn straws, you may buy a brand new Broom Corn (not plastic) broom or whisk, fill your bathtub with warm water, and "sweep" the broom or whisk through the water. White Mustard seeds can be added to such a bath, and you can substitute a pinch of powdered Mustard from your kitchen, or even a bit of prepared mustard — but not too much, because Mustard powder and prepared Mustard are stronger than Mustard seeds and can sting your skin.

BATHS FOR PROTECTION

Spiritual baths are used for protection from physical danger and negativity or to ward off magical attacks, evil influences, and unwanted spirits. The regular use of protective baths can reduce the amount of uncrossing needed, as protection keeps your life "mess-free."

- **Devil's Shoe String Bath Crystals:** Ties up (or ties down!) unwanted spirits and troublesome people.
- **Fear Not to Walk Over Evil Bath Crystals:** To protect against foot-track magic or tricks laid on the ground.
- **Fiery Wall of Protection Bath Crystals:** Strong, hot protection against all forms of evil; it may cause pain to wrongdoers.
- **Law Keep Away Bath Crystals:** For protection of any business that may be subject to legal or police scrutiny, deserved or undeserved.
- **Protection Bath Crystals:** A cool and clear protection from bad influences; it is quite calming as well as protective.
- **Reversing Bath Crystals:** Used to send a jinx, hex, or crossed conditions back to the sender.
- **Rue Bath Crystals:** For protection against the evil eye of jealousy.
- **Run Devil Run Bath Crystals:** To drive away evil spirits, demons, and devils, including those in human form.
- **Safe Travel Bath Crystals:** For protection of the person on a journey or vacationing as well as of the home during the absence.

PROTECTIVE BAY LEAF BATH
A soaking bath for protection that requires no advance preparation is easily made with nothing more than Bay leaves, a capful of Chinese Wash, and a tablespoon of salt. Stir them into the bath, letting the Bay leaves float, and recite the 91st and 121st Psalms.

A PERSONAL PROTECTION WASH
(from *Hoodoo Herb and Root Magic* by catherine yronwode)
Boil Basil in water, strain out the leaves, and wipe yourself downward with a white handkerchief dipped in the water. Do this every morning for nine days. On the last day, throw the remaining bath water out your front door, and your enemies cannot harm you.

HAIR RINSE FOR PROTECTION OF THE MIND

Make a tea of Mint and Sage. Strain it, let it cool and rinse your hair with the tea making sure to rub into the scalp. Let it dry in your hair.

HAIR RINSE TO KEEP FROM BEING HOODOOED

Make the rinse while the clock hands rise or during the waxing Moon, if possible, on a Monday. Warm a quart of Apple cider vinegar. In a glass jug, add the vinegar to 3 tablespoons each of Rue, Agrimony, and Sage (or Basil). Let steep for 2 weeks to a month. Strain out the herbs. Mix 1 part vinegar to 1 - 3 parts spring water and keep tightly bottled. To use, wash hair as usual and then finish with 1/2 cup of the rinse poured over the hair and left to dry. Not only will the herbs reverse any magic done using your hair, this wash also breaks hexes and keeps the evil eye away.

RUE WATER CHARM AGAINST THE EVIL EYE

Make this on New Year's Day, as the Sun rises. Place Rue herb in a pretty glass jar with fresh spring water (or melted snow if you have it). Tie a ribbon around the neck of the bottle and keep it outside near the house or on a window sill. It will protect against the evil eye throughout the year.

HEALING WASH FOR TOWEL BATHING IN THE SICK ROOM

Mix 1 part Althea to heal and soothe, 1 part Slippery Elm bark to keep evil away, 1/4 part Flax seed meal for healing and protection, 1/8 part Blessed Thistle for protection and healing, and 1/8 part Yerba Santa for healing and spiritual aid. As needed, infuse a dilute tea (3 tablespoons of herbal mix to 4 cups of water) in a covered container for half an hour. Strain through cheese cloth, squeezing out all of the mucilage that you can. Apply as a towel-bath and pay special attention to the head, face, and feet when you do.

PROTECTION HAND AND FOOT WASH

If you suspect that false friends or co-workers have laid tricks for you, mix 1 part each of Slippery Elm bark, chopped-up Eucalyptus leaves, and Agrimony herb. You can store this mixture dry until use. As needed, boil 3 tablespoons of the herbs plus 1/4 packet of Protection Bath Crystals in 4 cups of water for 5 minutes. Strain out the herbs. Use the liquid to wash your hands and feet, to protect against tricked objects or pathways.

BATHS FOR LOVE AND SEX

Love work leads many people to the practice of magic. Baths for love are a great way to prepare for a date night or to attract romance as you ready yourself for an evening out on the town. When working for sexual attraction, it is customary to wash the genital area carefully, in essence laying a trick there for the desired lover.

Bath crystals for love and romance can be blended as you wish, in order to obtain exactly the effect desired. For instance, Love Me and Marriage are combined to engender a love affair and to bring the affair to the altar. Likewise, Return To Me is combined with Reconciliation to bring a lover home after a fight and to lead to forgiveness and an end to anger.

A drop or two of condition oil can also be added to any love or passion drawing or bath crystals or herbs to subtly modify their use in the same manner. For example, if you have Q Oil but no Q Bath Crystals, you can drizzle the Q Oil into your Kiss Me Now! Bath Crystals to mark them as being for a same-sex relationship that is hot, passionate, and lusty.

An old-fashioned word of advice with regards to spell timing when doing love work: To draw a long-term partner who will work hard for you all day, bathe as the Sun rises. If you try to draw a life-mate at night you will only attract those who will run around and leave you alone as the day ends.

Used water from an herbal love bath can be used to cook with in order to entice or win over a lover. If the bath contained mineral salts, it can't be used in cooking, but it can be used to fix a target's laundry, which is more effective than simply deploying it in the front or back yard or at a crossroads.

- **Adam and Eve Bath Crystals:** To help find a life-mate or soul-mate; to bring about natural love.
- **Bewitching Bath Crystals:** To be more alluring and fascinating: to be someone you just have to get to know.
- **Chuparrosa Bath Crystals:** To bring about a sincere, honest, loving, and long-lasting relationship.
- **Cleo May Bath Crystals:** To make men more financially generous to women who wear it; used by sex workers, but any woman in a service industry can use it to get tips and favours.
- **Come To Me Bath Crystals:** To attract a new lover or draw a known person closer.

- **Dixie Love Bath Crystals:** For family-love, to encourage a parent to care for children; to cause partners to be gently affectionate.
- **Essence of Bend-Over Bath Crystals:** For domination in love.
- **Fire of Love Bath Crystals:** Kindles passion. Particularly suited to existing relationships where the spark needs some help.
- **Follow Me Boy / Girl Bath Crystals:** To cause a person of the gender of choice to follow you and be entranced by your every move.
- **I Dominate My Man / Woman Bath Crystals:** To gain complete control over a lover in mind, body, and soul.
- **Jezebel Bath Crystals:** Used in the sex industry to attract wealthy clients; combines well with Cleo May.
- **King Solomon Wisdom Bath Crystals:** Brings about wise decisions in love. Solomon wrote passionate, beautiful verses about human love.
- **Kiss Me Now! Bath Crystals:** For quick sex; can be combined with Fire of Love to revive waning sexuality in an existing relationship.
- **Lavender Love Drops Bath Crystals:** To attract a same-sex lover; can be combined with Q for lust, or with Marriage for fidelity.
- **Look Me Over Bath Crystals:** To become the object of attention; combines well with Bewitching; it is also used in non-love situations.
- **Love Me Bath Crystals:** Used to obtain love from a specific person, especially for a long-time relationship.
- **Marriage Bath Crystals:** To attract a proposal of marriage and to reinforce love within an existing marriage.
- **Q Bath Crystals:** For homosexual men to find passion, love, and lust; the letter "Q" stands for "queer."
- **Reconciliation Bath Crystals:** For reconciliation and renewal of affection after an argument.
- **Return To Me Bath Crystals:** To bring back a lover who has left; also used on friends or family if needed.
- **Stay At Home Bath Crystals:** To keep a lover in the home with the family; also used on children who want to run around late at night.
- **Stay With Me Bath Crystals:** For commitment, for fidelity; and to prevent divorce.
- **Florida Water Cologne:** Splashed into the bath or used as an after-bath rubdown, it emanates a delightful, exiting scent.
- **Love Herbs Mixture:** A combination of love herbs dressed with love oils; it is used as a bathing tea or floor sprinkle for the bedroom.

FOR MORE PASSION IN AN EXISTING RELATIONSHIP
Make a custom blend of 1 packet each of Tranquility, King Solomon Wisdom, Nature, Fire of Love, and Kiss Me Now! bath crystals. Keep the mix in a fancy looking bottle by the tub to fix long soaky baths prior to bed. This will help ease stress and add a bit of "Luvin Vibe" to the water. A pinch of the same mix, added to wash water for socks and underwear, will work by contact with the clothes when they are worn.

TO STRENGTHEN AND PROTECT A RELATIONSHIP
Make a custom blend of bath crystals consisting of 1 packet each of Chuparrosa, Fire of Love, and King Solomon Wisdom bath crystals.

MISS TAMMIE LEE'S SUMMER LOVE SPRITZERS
Here are two different bath crystal blends. The first is for dating or quick sex, the second is for long-term love.
   • Attraction, Follow Me Boy (or Follow Me Girl), Fast Luck
   • Love Me, Fire of Love, Stay With Me, Dixie Love
Chose whichever combination you like, then mix equal parts of each product and store in a sealed jar. As needed, dissolve a small amount in water to make a lightly-scented spritzer you can carry in your purse.

TO GET LUCKY WHEN YOU'RE LOOKING FOR A PICK UP
Make a custom blend consisting of 1 part each of Look Me Over, Kiss Me Now!, and Fast Luck bath crystals. Bathe with this and use a pinch of the mixture in the wash water for the clothes you'll be wearing out.

TO ENCOURAGE A FEMALE LOVER TO RETURN
Mix 1 part each of Attraction, Follow Me Girl, and Return To Me bath crystals. If you are a man, add 1 part John the Conqueror bath crystals. If you are a woman, instead add 1 part Queen Elizabeth Root bath crystals.

HERB BATH TO DRAW A NEW LOVE
Bathe in a tea made of Juniper berries, Cubeb berries, and a chopped Vanilla bean. If you don't have a whole Vanilla bean, substitute 1/2 teaspoon of real Vanilla extract instead. Bathe upward. Throw the bath water into your front yard, to the East if possible, along with all the herbal material used in making the tea.

THE MARRIAGE BATH

If your lover will have sex, but is reluctant to marry, collect some of your remnant bath water from any beverage-safe all-herb love bath, your combined sexual fluids, and your period blood (if available). Store in the freezer until needed. Add small amounts to the cream sauce, dinner gravy, or creamed soups that you cook for your lover, praying for a wedding.

MARITAL FELICITY AND FIDELITY (FOR A WOMAN)

Mix 1 cup Raspberry leaf tea with 1 packet Stay With Me Bath Crystals.

HERBAL BLEND TO INCREASE FEMALE NATURE

This bath is safe to drink as a beverage. Combine 1 part Raspberry leaf, 1 part Red Clover tops, 1/4 part Rose buds, 1/4 part Ginger, and 1/8 part Cubeb berries. For use as a bath, infuse 4-6 tablespoons of the mixture per quart of water. To prepare as a beverage tea, use 1 teaspoon of the mixture per cup of hot water, and sweeten with honey, if you wish.

PAPA NEWT'S STRENGTH OF SAMPSON MALE BATH

Place 1 Sampson Snake Root, 3 Lovage root slices, 1 tablespoon Cardamon Seed, and 1 High John the Conqueror root in a quart of water and bring to a boil for seven minutes. Take off of heat, add 1 tablespoon Master of the Woods herb, and let it steep for 3 minutes. Pour the bath-tea mixture into a gallon bucket of warm water while straining out the roots and herbs.

SWEET BATH FOR COMPASSION AND A FAMILY BOND

To a full bath of warm water add 1 cup of whole milk, 1/4 cup of honey and 1 quart of fresh white Rose petal tea. This is a great bath to take as a couple and it is also a good first bath for a couple to take with their newborn child. It increases softness, sweetness, and compassion.

HONEY BATH FOR LOVE AND SWEETNESS

Take a bath in which you have diluted half a packet of Love Me bath crystals. Get out of the bath but do not empty the water. Air dry and then rub honey over your entire body from the feet up, concentrating on your petition. Sit back into the water and wash the honey off of your body. Leave the bath, air dry once more, and dispose of the bath water.

DEACON'S SUGARED HERB BATH TO DRAW NEW LOVE

(from "Hoodoo Honey and Sugar Spells" by Deacon Millett)
Combine 1 tablespoon of sugar, a handful of Rose petals, a handful of Lavender flowers, a pinch of Catnip, a handful of Red Clover flowers, a Cardamom pod, and a stick of Cinnamon into a strong tea to pour into your bath. Alternatively, place the ingredients in a muslin sack added to the hot running water of the bath. Bathe by the light of red candles.

LOVE HERBS MIXTURE

This is an all-purpose blend for drawing new love, increasing sexual passion, bringing about reconciliation, and sustaining fidelity. Combine equal parts Cardamom, Catnip, Cubebs, Damiana, Juniper berries, Rose petals, Red Clover tops, Cherry Bark, and Jasmine flowers. The mixture can be steeped for use in a bath as well as included in other spell work.

MISS CAT'S WAY TO GET ORAL SEX FROM A PARTNER

"Use some of the edible love herbs in his food, like Catnip, Damiana, Cardamom seeds, Juniper berries, and Grains of Paradise. Don't use so much herbal matter that he will notice, just put a little in his food along with other spices and herbs. As you stir the food, recite a portion from the Song of Solomon in the Bible. Do this for a few weeks.

"When you get your period, add a bit of your blood to the food with the herbs, all the while praying the Song of Solomon over the food. Save some of your period blood in the freezer and keep adding it to his food, along with the herbs. If you don't have periods, use your sexual fluids.

"Next add a routine of bathing in a tea that is made from those same love herbs mentioned above. After you have done this for about a month, if you still get no action, try washing his clothes in a tea made the same herbs, and add a sprinkle of Essence of Bend-Over Bath Crystals and Jezebel Bath Crystals to the laundry rinse water, always reciting the Song of Solomon over your work.

"I have used this method with success on a former lover who was completely opposed to oral pleasure either way, and he became quite interested in it both ways, to his surprise.

"If your partner is very stubborn, make a doll-baby of him, tell it, 'You will go where i send you!' and let it explore the areas where he needs to follow it to."

TO ADD HEAT OR PASSION TO ANY LOVE BATH

Add Ginger! Either dried, powdered, or freshly grated Ginger will work well; just don't add too much, as it can irritate the skin.

FIERY HOT BATH OF DESIRE

Mix 1 teaspoon each Cinnamon chips, crushed Juniper berries, and fresh chopped Ginger and boil them in a quart of water until the water is reduced to about 1 cup, making a strong decoction. Strain out the herbs and pour the liquid into a bottle that is 3/4 filled with Lanman and Kemp Rose Blossom Cologne; you may have enough to make two such bottles. Shake well. Just a splash of this combination will jump-start any mineral bath, milk bath, or honey bath and take it to a new level.

PAPA NEWTS'S LOVE MOLOTOV COCKTAIL BATH

Mix 1/4 pack each Look Me Over, Bewitching, Kiss Me Now!, and Love Me Bath Crystals to your bath water and soak in the mixture while praying for love or just for a good time, asking that it takes place that night. Air dry, get dressed, and have a fun night!

A MAN'S BATH FOR VITALITY, HEALTH, AND STRENGTH

Make a custom blend consisting of 1 packet John the Conqueror bath crystals, 1 packet Nature bath crystals, and 1/4 teaspoon Ginseng powder. Divide into 3 parts and use to take baths on 3 Tuesdays, before sunrise.

"HOT MAMA DOUCHE" TO MAKE MEN EAGER FOR SEX

(from "Hoodoo Herb and Root Magic" by catherine yronwode)
Soak Juniper berries in distilled vinegar for a month, strain, dilute with warm water, and use as a vaginal douche.

MISS MICHAELE'S LOVE-PRAYER BATH TRICKS

To influence someone for love, give them a gift of a picture in a frame. Take a love bath and use a little bath water as ink to write your love-prayer on a plain piece of paper. Dry it and slip it behind the picture. The prayer will be invisible when dry — but only to the physical eye. Alternatively, write a prayer in water-soluble ink, or even food coloring. Before bathing; take the paper with you into the tub, rinse the prayer right off into the water, and use the water to dress a gift you give to the one you love.

BATHS FOR MONEY DRAWING AND BUSINESS

Improving one's finances is a common purpose of rootwork. When money is not a worry, life runs more smoothly and a great degree of worry that can affect both morale and health is removed.

Baths are often used as a part of money drawing spells, usually at the start, to set the tone of the work. A money or business success bath can also be used as a way of preparing for an important event, such as a job interview, performance review, or business meeting.

It is also customary to make up floor and sidewalk washes to draw in customers and trade to a store, business location, or home office. Such washes may be prepared with remnant bath water from a money drawing bath, thus doubling the focus on financial wealth and success.

- **Attraction Bath Crystals:** A drawing formula useful for any purpose, it is excellent for bringing in money and attracting clients.
- **Boss Fix Bath Crystals:** To get your boss to give you a raise, promote you, or treat you better on the job.
- **Crown of Success Bath Crystals:** This success formula can be added to a more money-specific formula to foster career success.
- **Fast Luck Bath Crystals:** Used when quick results are required, it may be combined with more money-specific formulas, as well as with any other drawing products that are slower but longer lasting.
- **King Solomon Wisdom Bath Crystals:** This may be added to money formulas so that the business decisions you make will be wise.
- **Money Drawing Bath Crystals:** To draw money in through business ventures, entrepreneurial endeavours, gifts, and lucky fortune.
- **Money House Blessing Bath Crystals:** To keep the home prosperous; combines well with Money Stay With Me and Prosperity formulas.
- **Money Stay With Me Bath Crystals:** To keep the money that you earn from disappearing; to curb spending and sustain durable goods.
- **Pay Me Bath Crystals:** For the return of money owed, to secure a promised fee, or to collect a legally mandated financial settlement.
- **Prosperity Bath Crystals:** To increase earnings and savings; useful when dealing with investments and retirement funds.
- **Wealthy Way Bath Crystals:** To bring about enough cash flow for society's luxuries and status symbols.

FINANCIAL UNCROSSING BATH

Combine Pine Needles, Basil, and Sage for use as a bath or floor wash. This combination will uncross and cleanse away financial poverty and negativity, draw in money abundantly, and help you to spend it wisely.

HEAL AND IMPROVE HOME FINANCES BATH BLEND

Boil up a pot of water and add Fenugreek seeds, Irish Moss, Alfalfa, Mallow (Althaea) root, and salt. Add to the bath weekly or use a quarter cup of the tea in the wash water for the house every week. Dispose of the remains over the side-walk leading to the home.

MONEY-T FOR PROSPERITY AND BUSINESS SUCCESS

Make an herbal blend consisting of 1/2 cup Yellow Dock root, 3/4 cup Sassafrass root, 1 stick Cinnamon, 3 teaspoons whole Cloves, and 1 teaspoon Allspice berries. Cut or crush the larger items to a uniform texture, so you can measure the mixture out. On a Thursday or Friday, as the clock hands rise, or before sunrise, prepare your bath with 3 tablespoons of the herbs in 3 cups of spring water. Simmer on the stove-top, covered, for 21 minutes and strain. Add it to your bath and soak for 21 minutes. As you bathe, close your eyes and visualize prosperity in your life. Make sure to wash your face with the water and if your hairstyle permits, pour some water over your head. Pray Psalms 23. When you're done bathing, keep a cup of the used bath water that now has your essence in it. Add that water to the scrub water for your apartment, house, and/or business when you clean the floors.

COIN WASH

Collect a double handful of shiny, brand-new coins in assorted denominations. Prepare a bath-tea with equal parts whole Cloves, Allspice Berries, and Blue Flag Root, plus a drop of honey. Strain the tea into a wash basin, and "wash" each coin between your hands as you pray Psalms 23. Let the coins dry on a clean, white cloth. When you go out in the streets, distribute the coins to the poor, for as it says in Deuteronomy 15:7: "If there be among you a poor man of one of thy brethren within any of thy gates in thy land which the Lord thy God giveth thee, thou shalt not harden thine heart, nor shut thine hand from thy poor brother." For this good deed, you will be blessed.

BATHS FOR GAMBLING LUCK

There is a long tradition of using baths and washes to help bring in luck and winnings from betting and games of chance. Full baths can be taken before going to play, but often a wash will be made and used to dress the only hands when the goal is to improve your play at cards or at the casino.

- **Aunt Sally's Lucky Dream Bath Crystals:** To dream of lucky numbers to bet; a favourite with those who play policy or the numbers.
- **Black Cat Bath Crystals:** To bring money luck, increase gambling luck, and, when a situation is risky, for "reverse bad luck."
- **Fast Luck Bath Crystals:** For rapid-action gambling games like slots, bingo, or roulette, where money moves quickly.
- **Five Finger Grass Bath Crystals:** For luck at games where the hands must be nimble, such as shooting dice.
- **Good Luck Bath Crystals:** To draws luck in love and money as well as success in all aspects of life.
- **Lady Luck Bath Crystals:** The choice of many women who go to the casinos to play bingo, keno, or the slots.
- **Lucky 13 Bath Crystals:** To generate good luck from bad conditions, for lottery play when there are at best long odds of winning.
- **Lucky Buddha Bath Crystals:** For luck and monetary wealth, used in tandem with Lucky Hotei Buddha statuary.
- **Lucky Hand Bath Crystals:** Very popular as a hand wash; used by gamblers before playing any game.
- **Lucky Mojo Bath Crystals:** For horse races, lotto, sweepstakes, and other games of chance.
- **Lucky Number Bath Crystals:** For determining numbers to bet, such as those selected from a dream book or through numerology.
- **Three Jacks and a King Bath Crystals:** To improve skill and luck at cards and in other games of chance.
- **Gambler's Gold Lucky Seven Hand Wash:** An herbal hand wash or bath used prior to all forms of gambling to help bring in the winnings.
- **Hoyt's Cologne:** Used as a perfume or aftershave to win in all kinds of games of chance.
- **Seven Herb Bath:** Herbal bath to draw luck in love, life, money, and games of chance.

ALL-HERB LUCKY HAND WASH

Chamomile is known as a soothing and calming tea, but the bright golden centers of its flowers also bring to mind the lure of gold. Alfalfa, the same kind we feed to cows and horses, is a symbol of never-ending money-luck. Five-Finger Grass is used to gain mastery in anything that your five fingers can do. Brew a bath-tea of equal parts of these three herbs and use it to wash your hands before you go to play cards, shoot dice, or engage in any form of gambling where the movement of your hands can help you to win.

GAMBLER'S LUCKY BATH

Mix a packet of your favourite of the prepared bath crystals for lucky gambling with a pinch of sugar, a pinch of powdered Cinnamon, and a splash of Hoyt's cologne. Bathe upward with the combination, paying special attention to the hands and head. Use Hoyt's as an aftershave.

HOYT'S COLOGNE SPECIAL BATH BLEND

To make this special bathing mix you will need to use a large-size bottle of Hoyt's Cologne until it is half-gone — that is, until the bottle is half-empty. Now top the bottle up with a blend of a few of your favourite gambling condition oils, such as Fast Luck Oil, Black Cat Oil, and Lucky Number Oil. Add to this bottle several pieces of pyrite grit that have been ground to powder, a pinch of magnetic sand, and a pinch of anvil dust. Shake the mixture up once a day for one week. After that you can shake it up and add a bit to your bath. Decant it slowly and carefully so as not to get the minerals into the bath water.

EMERGENCY GAMBLING BATH OR HAND WASH

If you have no spiritual supplies on hand at all — no lucky bath crystals, no Hoyt's Cologne, and not even any gamblers' lucky condition oils to drizzle into your bath — you can make an emergency gambler's bath and hand wash with Pumpkin Pie Spice from the grocery store. Most brands of Pumpkin Pie Spice contain herbs like Cinnamon, Allspice, and Nutmeg, all of which are well known as gambler's herbs. Boil 1/4 teaspoon of the Pumpkin Pie Spices in a pot of water, add a pinch of sugar, strain or carefully decant the liquid, and you have a very decent gambler's bath or lucky hand wash.

BATHS FOR BLESSINGS AND SUCCESS

Blessing baths can be performed for yourself or you may seek out a hands-on healer to perform a head rub to clear your mind or a blessing of the hands to further your success. A home practitioner may give a blessing bath to a family member to bestow success; mothers often do so on their children. Blessing bath-teas may be used to dress gift items destined for a target. For instance, gifts of clothing or bedding can be washed in prepared water. To bless a location for success, dilute bath crystals in the wash water used on the floors and walls.

- **Blessing Bath Crystals:** Pretty self-explanatory; the type of blessings you request can be mentioned by name as you pray.
- **Crown of Success Bath Crystals:** For career, school and business success. Great as a head wash.
- **Crucible of Courage Bath Crystals:** Encourages courage, bravery, and determination; helps in difficult situations and for taming fear.
- **Five Finger Grass Bath Crystals:** When manual dexterity is required; used in hand-blessings, it is also protective and luck-bringing.
- **House Blessing Bath Crystals:** To bless the home and family with happiness, health, and prosperity.
- **John The Conqueror Bath Crystals:** Increases charisma, vitality, strength and mastery.
- **King Solomon Wisdom Bath Crystals:** Often used for school success and academic ventures.
- **Money House Blessing Bath Crystals:** To bring the blessings of financial stability to the home.
- **Peony Root Bath Crystals:** Safeguards and improves health and luck. Has a very sweet energy.
- **Spirit Guide Bath Crystals:** An appeal to a guardian spirit to show the way forward and to bring messages from the other side.
- **Tranquility Bath Crystals:** For peace of mind, an end to doubts, and peace in the heart.

BATH FOR SCHOOL SUCCESS

Combine one part each King Solomon Wisdom and Crown of Success bath crystals with a good-size pinch of dried Peach tree leaves.

CONJUREMAN ALI'S BATH FOR FERTILITY

Make a bath out of Squaw Vine, Queen Elizabeth Root, and Rosemary. Bathe with it for 7 days at Sunrise, taking the used water to the crossroads and praying for the ability to conceive and carry a healthy baby to term as you toss the water to the rising Sun.

BATH TO BLESS A NEWBORN

Add a strong tea of fresh white Roses and fresh or dried Chamomile to the bath. This surrounds the young spirit with love and luck. Bathe the child upward.

BLESSING A NEW HOME

Get to the new home on the day you will be moving in, significantly before the Sun rises. Rinse out the bath with a combination of salt, vinegar, and baking soda. Draw a hot bath with a combination of House Blessing, Money Stay With Me, and Peaceful Home bath crystals. Bathe, pouring the combination over your head (or immersing yourself fully into the tub) and praying Psalms 23. Add some of the used bath water and a pinch of sugar to a bucket of wash water and mop the new home from top to bottom and from back to front. Mop out the front door and pour the water out along the front steps, the walk to the home, or into the front yard. Everything should be completed as the Sun is rising.

FIXING CLOTHING FOR THE SUCCESS OF A MUSICIAN

Boil a John the Conqueror root in a quart of water for 9 minutes. Add Five Finger grass, magnetic sand or anvil dust that has laid long on a money drawing lodestone, an Allspice berry, and Deer's Tongue to the tea. Let steep for another 9 minutes. Strain the water and use it as a wash for a piece of clothing to be given to the musician. You can also put the tea into a spray-bottle and use it to fix hats, shoes, or instrument cases, or to wash the hands before a show.

MARRIAGE BLESSINGS BATH

Make a tea with a handful each of Honeysuckle flowers, Jasmine flowers, Passionflower, Lavender flowers and a large Spikenard root. Add the tea to a warm bath either prior to the wedding or during the honeymoon.

BATHS AND WASHES FOR BEAUTY AND GLAMOUR

Baths and herbal waters have historically been used to improve appearance and maintain beauty, and it's not for nothing that a mythical fountain is said to exist that bestows eternal youth! Spas today continue to abound, offering hydrotherapeutic procedures of an almost magical nature. Bathing products and special waters used when working for beauty and glamour may also be blended with products for romance and love.

- **Attraction Bath Crystals:** To draw attention to yourself
- **Bewitching Bath Crystals:** To fascinate and beguile others.
- **Dove's Blood Bath Crystals:** For a humble, submissive appearance.
- **Look Me Over Bath Crystals:** To get attention from those around you.
- **Magnet Bath Crystals:** To cause someone to cling to you with the obsessive interest exemplified by metal clinging to a magnet.
- **Nature Bath Crystals:** To increase nature and sexual vitality.
- **Peony Root Bath Crystals:** For health, longevity, and glowing youth.
- **Queen Elizabeth Root Bath Crystals:** For women who are working to come to terms with their power, nature, health and appearance.
- **Florida Water Cologne:** The label shows the fabled fountain of youth; the scent is described as refreshing, revitalizing, and exhilarating.
- **Orange Blossom Water:** Makes an excellent astringent for the skin, particularly for those doing marriage work.
- **Rose Water:** Makes an excellent astringent for the skin, particularly for those doing love work.

COSMETIC WASH TO PRESERVE YOUTHFUL FEATURES
(from "Hoodoo Herb and Root Magic" by catherine yronwode)
An old cosmetic wash that is said to help preserve youthful features consists of nothing more complicated than Rosemary soaked for 3 days in pure spring water. This is strained and used to wash the face both morning and night.

DEVI SPRING'S FACIAL SPRITZ
In a dark glass spray bottle combine 2 parts Rose water and 1 part Witch Hazel with 13 drops of Frankincense essential oil. It's fantastic for the complexion and smells divine too!

"QUEEN OF HUNGARY'S WATER" HERBAL TONER

This is a very old recipe and there are many variations of it. Mix together the following herbs, either fresh or dried: 6 parts Lemon Balm (Melissa), 4 parts Chamomile, 1 part Rosemary, 3 parts Calendula, 4 parts fragrant Roses, 1 part Sage leaves, and 3 parts Comfrey leaves. You will also need vinegar (usually red wine or Apple cider vinegar) and/or Witch Hazel extract, Rose water, and a small amount of Rose essential or fragrance oil and/or a small amount of Lavender essential oil. Begin the day after the New Moon. Mix all the herbs in a jar and cover over with either the Witch Hazel extract or vinegar, or a blend of the two. There should be 1-2 inches of liquid above the herbs. Let steep during the waxing Moon. If the herbs were dried, they will swell, and you may have to add more vinegar to keep the herbs submerged. Strain off on the day of the Full Moon. To each cup of the strained liquid add half a cup of Rose Water, plus a drop or two of either Rose or Lavender essential oil, or both. Bottle and keep in a dark place, using as a facial toner when necessary. This product does not need to be refrigerated.

MADAME NADIA'S GOLD DIGGER BODY SCRUB

According to Madame Nadia, this delicious enchantment is designed to attract the attention of patrons who are interested in showering you with gifts and supporting you financially. On a cosmetic level, this scrub will do wonders to your skin, smoothing and nourishing it. Mix together 1/2 cup white cane sugar, 1/2 cup Sweet Almond oil, 1 1/2 tablespoons Goldschläger or Fireball Whisky, a pinch each of Calendula, Five-Finger Grass, and Catnip (if you're a female) or Calamus (if you are a male), plus 2 drops of Sweet Orange essential Oil, 2 drops of Chamomile essential Oil, and 1 dropper-full each of Follow Me Boy (or Follow Me Girl), Look Me Over, Bewitching, and Cleo May condition oils. Work everything together and use it to scrub your body from foot to head, drawing in sexual fascination and financial generosity.

DEACON MILLETT'S SEDUCTION SUGAR BATH

Crush a handful of dried Juniper berries with sugar and add a small amount of chopped fresh Ginger root. Gay men, add a half-handful of Safflower petals to the mix; women, add Roses. Boil a few minutes and strain for use in the bath. This will heat up your evening.

BATHS AND WASHES FOR A PEACEFUL HOME

Baths and washes are an excellent way to maintain peace, joy, and equanimity in the home. They can clean away the residue from a bad fight, remove the negativity following an unexpected visit from unpleasant in-laws, and generally make the home an inviting haven of rest and relaxation for the entire family. Consider adding them, unannounced, to regular household cleaning supplies, such as Chinese Wash.

- **Blessing Bath Crystals:** Often chosen when moving into a new home to bless the building's future and also its inhabitants.
- **Clarity Bath Crystals:** To see relationships within the family clearly.
- **Dixie John Bath Crystals:** For luck, love, and agreeable family relationships. A great all-round house wash and bathing mixture; it combines well with House Blessing.
- **House Blessing Bath Crystals:** To bless the home and family with happiness, health, and prosperity.
- **Money House Blessing Bath Crystals:** Keeps the home prosperous. Combines well with Money Stay With Me and Prosperity formulas.
- **Peaceful Home Bath Crystals:** The classic formula for maintaining a home that is calm, happy, and welcoming.
- **Tranquility Bath Crystals:** To calm agitation and bring peace.
- **Peace Water:** Sprinkled in the home to draw in only kind people and good intentions. Great for family reunions.
- **Peaceful Home Herbs Mixture:** Multi-purpose combination of oil-dressed herbs for home fidelity and happiness. Can be used as a bathing tea or floor sprinkle.

RESPECT YOUR MOMMA BATH AND WASHING BLEND
Make a tea from 1 teaspoon of Blood Root chips and a handful each of Rosemary and Motherwort. Add some of the tea to the bath water for the children and some to the wash water for their bedrooms and bed-clothes.

PROTECT THE LOVE IN THE HOME HERBAL BLEND
Combine equal parts dried Rue, Rose petals and Lavender blossoms. To help the woman of the house have more sway, Rosemary can also be added. For a bit more peace in the home, add Borage.

MISS BRI'S EASTER FLOOR WASH

"This is a variation of a floor wash that both Momma Hen (my mother) and I use at Easter time. Easter cleaning is a tradition in our Texas households that has both spiritual and practical significance.

"You will need 3 Balm of Gilead buds, 1 packet Peaceful Home Herbs mix, 7 drops Jesus Christ the King oil, a splash of 7-11 Holy Oil, 1 whole Angelica root, and 3-5 slices of Jezebel root if you have it (the Jezebel root addition started with my Nanna — she said it was to honor Mary Magdalene, and that was all she said).

"On the morning of the Friday before Easter (Good Friday) steep all of the herbs and roots in hot water for 21 minutes, strain all herbs and roots out, and allow the water to cool. Add the oils, praying the Lord's Prayer over the water as you do so.

"Clean your home with the water as you normally would, back to front and ceiling to floor. If you wish to light a small white candle in each room as you finish up you may do so, anointing it with some of the Jesus Christ the King oil.

"The house cleaning can be done any time between Friday afternoon and Sunday dinner or it can be spread out over Friday, Saturday, and Sunday."

ALL-PURPOSE BATH CRYSTAL COMBO FOR THE HOME

Mix Dixie John, Tranquility, and Peaceful Home bath crystals in a fancy un-marked glass jar. Tie pretty blue, pink, and white ribbons around the jar. Use this to fix relaxing tricked baths for family members, and also dissolve some of the crystals to add to your laundry, specifically socks, underwear, and bed linens.

FOR PEACE IN THE HOME

Boil a pack of Peaceful Home Herbs in a gallon of water. Strain out the herbs. Get a few stalks of fresh Rosemary and fresh Basil and tie them into a bundle. Whisk the water with the herbs while praying for peace, plenty, and prosperity in the home. Dilute the tea into a bath of warm water, also reserving some for use in the laundry. To dispose of your remnant bath water, carry it outside and walk around the building, dipping the herb-bundle into the water and sprinkling bath-tea at every corner. When you are done, untie the herbs and scatter them around the yard.

FREQUENTLY ASKED QUESTIONS

The Lucky Mojo Forum was begun in 2008. Averaging 60 posts per day, it is an online community in which questions are answered daily with regards to the practice of hoodoo and the use of Lucky Mojo spiritual supplies. The Forum is open to all, and anyone can join and ask questions. The Lucky Mojo Forum can be accessed online at
Forum.LuckyMojo.com

Answers to questions, be they in the form of advice, encouragement, clarification, or spell suggestions, are provided by both forum members and a dedicated team of moderators who are all graduates of catherine yronwode's Hoodoo Rootwork Correspondence Course.
Read more about the Hoodoo Rootwork Correspondence Course at
LuckyMojo.com/mojocourse.html

The Frequently Asked Questions — and answers — that follow have been selected from a voluminous body of information at the Forum regarding hoodoo spiritual bathing practices. The record contained in the following pages is intended to complete and augment the information included in the preceding pages. If a question you have on spiritual bathing hasn't been answered yet, it should be by the time you reach the end of the book!

When reading the answers to the questions provided, note that user-names followed by an (M) are people who are or were at one time Forum moderators. Those marked (M, AIRR) are moderators who are also in professional practice and members of the Association of Independent Readers and Rootworkers:

catherine yronwode	Dr. Johannes
ConjureMan Ali	Lukianos
Deacon Millett	Miss Bri
Devi Spring	Leah Rivera
Miss Michaele	Mary Bee

AIRR members can be reached for personal readings, rootwork, magical coaching, and other professional services at the AIRR web site:
ReadersAndRootworkers.org

• **When and for how many days do I do a spiritual house cleaning?**

I want to know how many days I have to do the spiritual house cleaning and when it is appropriate to do it.

—theusurper

Depends on what you are doing it for. If it's just for general spiritual cleansing, then you can do it whenever you feel like it. You can just add some to your regular mop water. If you are using it as part of a larger uncrossing or cleansing work, then it would depend on the nature and length of that work.

—Devi Spring (M, AIRR)

Do it right before dawn on a day when the Moon is decreasing. If you are doing a strong cleansing, three times a week every third week for three months would be a good suggestion. It will establish a nice spiritually clean foundation in your home and thus make it harder for nasty spirits, negativity, and jinxes to get a grip there.

—Dr Johannes (M, AIRR)

This is what some folks do:

1) Do a full deep cleaning (top to bottom, back to front, getting into all the corners, wiping down the baseboards, etc.) once a year, praying while you go, and lighting a white candle in each room as your finish it. Such a process could take a couple days if the house is large and the cleaning crew small. The old wash water still goes out the front door (and preferably off the property) when you are done -- don't worry about whether it is before sunrise or considerably after.

2) On a daily or weekly basis, do a smaller cleaning in the morning (sweep or mop the public-area floors, for example) back to front, with prayer, and with the wash water going out the front door or off the property. This does not have to be before sunrise, unlike a personal spiritual bath, which would be done before sunrise if at all possible. You might set aside a span of time each day or week for cleaning and rotate areas to be cleaned; or you may have areas that are cleaned regularly versus others that are cleaned less often.

—Lukianos (M, AIRR)

• My house has two entrances; how can I tell which is the "front"?

I've read about house cleaning back to front, but what about when the home is generally entered from the back? The front faces the street and provides the address, but the alley is where everyone parks and enters.
—EleckticMama

You could go by the "address" as the front, or you could wash from the middle toward each exit, because technically you do use both entrances.
—Literarylioness (M)

• How do I dispose of the water used in spiritual house cleaning?

Should the water used to cleanse the house be disposed at a crossroads or can just a portion be taken there? My house is fairly large and I can't see lugging a huge pail to the crossroads as I have to walk there!
—CherryRedBoom

I take a small portion to the crossroads, but I dump the bulk of the water off of my property, usually out into the public street.
—Devi Spring (M, AIRR)

Scrub water buckets are easy to carry and dump into the gutter or ditch off of your property. Lucky Mojo brand Chinese Wash and 13-Herb Bath are non-toxic and non-polluting. I consider crossroads disposal unnecessary.
—catherine yronwode (M, AIRR)

• Must the whole house be washed on the same day?

I have a very large house. Do I need to do the whole house in one day? If I do the top floor one day and dispose of the water, and make a new bucket of water the next day and do the bottom floor, is that okay?
—babygirl

You can work over the course of several days. We do so here at our shop, every year.
—catherine yronwode (M, AIRR)

• What are the best cleansing practices for a new home?

My husband and I will be moving to another apartment soon, and it needs a little work. The owner said that the previous tenants left because they were fighting and had split up. Do you have any suggestions on how to remove the possible negative energies left behind, so we can start fresh?
—Angelina

Whenever my husband and I move to a new space I follow the tradition of leaving my old broom at the old place and buying a new broom for the first sweeping of the new place.

I love using Chinese Wash, and after mopping out with the Chinese Wash, you can usher in the good by doing a drawing wash with a combination of Money House Blessing and Peaceful Home bath crystals.

If you are still worried about the vibe of the your apartment, then after cleaning I would light a Peaceful Home vigil and put it in a prominent place, like on a mantle or in a central room.
—Miss Bri (M, AIRR)

• Should house cleaning be done for 13 successive days?

Is it traditional to wash the house during all the 13 days of a series of 13-Herb baths? I figured on doing it the first and last day but wasn't sure.
—CherryRedBoom

The practice of bathing thirteen days in a row is for bathing your body, and is usually only undertaken if you have had a serious run of bad luck or have a known enemy. The idea of being bathed for 13 days does bring to mind the lyrics of the old song "Black Cat Bone" as sung by K. C. Douglas, and recorded in Oakland, California, in 1972:
For thirteen days she run to the hoodoo man
Yeah, for thirteen days she run to the hoodoo man
When she come back home, everything was under her command.
13-Herb Bath can be added to house scrub water, or used alone as a floor or house wash, but, generally speaking, you would not scrub your house for 13 days in a row unless it was haunted or a murder had taken place there.
—catherine yronwode (M, AIRR)

• Are there benefits to cleaning the walls as well as the floors?

What are the reasons and benefits of cleansing the walls of the home rather than just the floors?
—blueberry

Washing the walls is part of a very thorough spiritual house cleansing performed for a long-standing condition, or when doing a yearly deep-clean. This step is often omitted in maintenance-type cleaning activities.
—Devi Spring (M, AIRR)

It's traditional to wash the walls as well as the floors of a vacant rental unit in order to attract renters.
—catherine yronwode (M, AIRR)

• How do I cleanse a carpeted floor?

I'm going to be moving into a new apartment and I am using a floor wash on the hardwood floors, walls, and ceilings. However, the apartment has mostly carpeted floors; how would I go about cleansing those?
—Deffy

You can use a floor wash on the carpeted floors. Just spray the floor lightly using a dilute mixture of bath crystals and water in a spray bottle and sweep with a broom out the door. Make sure it's a new broom since you are moving into a new place.
—starsinthesky7 (M)

I like to take baking soda (which is cleansing by itself) and mix it with a few drops of a cleansing or blessing oil. Then I sprinkle it on the carpet and vacuum. Another way to make floor sprinkles for different conditions is by either adding sachet powder or bath crystals to baking soda.
—Mama Micki (M)

If you have time before moving in, steam clean the carpets and add some of the Chinese Wash to the soapy water the steamer uses.
—Maljen

• **Different sets of tools for regular and spiritual house cleaning?**

Do you have two sets of separate broom and cleaning supplies, one set for spiritual cleansing and another set for regular cleaning, or do you use the same supplies for both purposes? Do you throw out your cleaning supplies, like the broom and mop, after you do a spiritual cleansing?

—corazon

Let's look at the history: Hoodoo is African American folk magic and for hundreds of years, African Americans were slaves and then servants. Only recently have they taken their place as equals under law with white Americans. Due to these conditions, they were kept in poverty and want.

Now let's ask the obvious question: Would the folk magic of a community that lived frugally, due to widespread economic discrimination and hardship, include such WASTE as throwing away a wash cloth every time it was used to cleanse or keep two sets of cleaning tools in the house? The answer is obviously, "No."

The idea of discarding a mop or a broom after one house cleaning is ridiculous to me. It is conspicuous consumption, a waste of resources, a financial drain, and a uselessly baroque "rule" that has been added to or conflated with the much older rule to use a new broom when you move to a new house. However, once you purchase that new broom for the new house, it becomes your "regular" broom until it is all worn out.

Most practitioners clean their house with spiritual supplies regularly. If you get into the groove of always using spiritual supplies to clean up, you will not even think about buying extra tools.

—catherine yronwode (M, AIRR)

People don't get rid of their tools after a spiritual cleaning; mops can get expensive, after all! Some cleanse the tools with a spray of Florida Water or a dilute spritz of Chinese Wash and hot water. Some don't cleanse the tools at all, they just rinse them out, considering that the product they used to do the cleansing did the job!

—aura (M)

No. You can keep your cleaning tools and use them again.

—jwmcclin (M)

• How can I use bath crystals in a front loading washer?

Has anyone used the bath crystals in an energy efficient front loading washer? Where did you put them — in the drum with the clothes themselves or in the detergent dispenser? I love all the herb and root chunks but am afraid they'll get stuck in the lines.
— Liz_H

There are two easy ways to use bath crystals in a washing machine. One is to add a pinch of the crystals to the rinse cycle of the wash. You open the door a bit, pray quick over your crystals, throw them in, and shut the door. The second method, which may work better in your particular machine, is to dissolve the crystals in hot water and add the water to your detergent; that way whenever you use the detergent you're doing the spell.
— MaryBee (M, AIRR)

When I had a front-loading washer, I increased the water level to the highest it would go and added a drop of Chinese Wash with my detergent in the little tray that slides out. With my washer, you had to put everything in that little tray before the wash program began: soap, softener, bleach, magical products. I assume the one you are using works the same way. So for the bath crystals, try making a tea and pour a little into the detergent or softener holder of that little tray before you begin the wash cycle.
— MoonBreath

• Can I use bath crystals to make a room spray?

Would it be all right to dissolve bath crystals (say, Van Van, Tranquility, or Fiery Wall of Protection, for example) in water and put the water into a spray bottle to use as a spray or spritzer around the house?
— giovanna_1530

Sure. You will want to strain the liquid first, however, so that any herb or root pieces present in the bath crystal mixture don't clog the orifice of the spray bottle. Some people also enjoy adding a couple of drops of condition oil as well and then shaking up the emulsion just prior to use.
— MaryBee (M, AIRR)

• Is there a wrong way to bathe?

Is there a wrong way to do a spiritual bath?

— MojoGuy365

Yes, there are "wrong" ways to prepare a bath. One "wrong" way would be to use toxic or skin irritant herbs in concentrated (undiluted) form. Another "wrong" way would be to use herbs or roots that do not accord with your intention when considered on the basis of their traditional spiritual usages. There are other "wrong" ways as well. For example, adding "whatever you like" is not a good idea.

Here are some "right" ways: To learn the properties of the materials you are working with, purchase a copy of my book "Hoodoo Herb and Root Magic." For sweet baths made with milk, see Deacon Millett's book "Hoodoo Honey and Sugar Spells." It will open your eyes.

— catherine yronwode (M, AIRR)

• Can I take a spiritual bath if I don't have a bathtub?

Unfortunately I do not have a bathtub, but a standup shower. Are there any suggestions about using any of the bath supplies in the shower?

— Ginger777

A lot of people have the situation that you are describing — no tub, only a shower. You can use one container that is full of the spiritual bath which you pour over yourself and then have another basin or bowl to catch some of the water that runs off of your body for ritual disposal You can pour several times (I prefer an odd number), praying as you do so. I have been in this situation before and it works just fine.

— Miss Bri (M, AIRR)

Spiritual baths are generally not really "tub baths," as most do not involve soaking. It's just generally more convenient to use a tub to stand in. Put a small tub-style container in your shower stall. Pour the bath down over yourself, or upwards on yourself, depending on the condition bath that you're taking. Collect some of that used bath water from the tub for use or disposal.

— Devi Spring (M, AIRR)

• Should I soak in the bath or pour it over my head?

When I take a spiritual bath, I usually just add the ingredients in the tub and soak, instead of pouring over my head. Does it have to be poured?
—lmlvr

Different people have different styles. Most people pour and do not soak. Remember, this is not soapy water — it is an herbal-mineral blend. Also, these customs originated long before bath tubs or indoor plumbing.
—catherine yronwode (M, AIRR)

• Can I take a spiritual bath if I can't soak in the water?

My gynecologist has told me to avoid baths, as I'm prone to urinary tract infections. I've been able to take short baths without a problem, but really soaking for a while can definitely trigger something. So, due to this health constraint, should I take faster baths when using bath products or should I convert everything to a shower, and only use the soaps I can lather with?
—LilCassandra

You can make an effective bath standing up and pouring the water over your body; there is no need for soaking. In fact, pouring is far more traditional than soaking. If you are very sensitive, have a bucket of bath water and portion that water over you. That way none of the water will be reused. This is effective if thrush or bacterial vaginosis is also an issue.
—Miss Ida Lundin (M)

• Can I use tap water to prepare a spiritual bath?

I will be taking a spiritual bath as part of a love spell. Is it okay to use tap water? If so, is there a special way to purify it?
—brteeyes01

Rather than use tap water, I suggest that you go the store, buy yourself a bottle of pure spring water, and use that to prepare your bath.
—Devi Spring (M, AIRR)

• **Do I have to pour the spiritual bath over my hair?**

I live in the Midwest where it is super dry and any moisture indoors simply evaporates. I have thick hair that takes forever to dry, even with a blow dryer. Would it be okay to put my hair inside a bathing cap so it doesn't get wet?

—ablake

Actually, no matter where you live, if you have a hair-do that you do not wish to get wet, it is just as traditional to wash the face and then from the neck downward. Also, different textures of hair require different approaches to showering and bathing, as most of the ladies here will testify.

Do not ever let someone tell you that there is only one "right" way to bathe. There are several "right" ways — and washing the face and then pouring or wiping from the neck down is old and traditional.

—catherine yronwode (M, AIRR)

• **Can I blow-dry my hair after a spiritual bath?**

When one is told to air dry after a spiritual bath, is it okay to let the body air dry and then dry one's hair with a dryer?

—rs09

I have lots of hair and I have found it acceptable to blow-dry my hair after bathing; you just don't wanna towel it off first. You can also drag a space heater to the bathroom and air dry in heat as well. The point is just to keep the water on your person so that it dries on you.

—Miss Bri (M, AIRR)

I have a ton of hair as well. Usually, I'm bathing early enough that I have time to let my hair dry for a few hours and then finish off the remaining moisture with a blow-dryer if I need to. I haven't found that this dampens the effect of the bath at all. There's always the option of bathing from the neck down if getting your hair wet is a problem, but I have to say, I love starting with the head. The scent lingers in your hair all day, and getting the occasional whiff is a continuous pick-me-up.

—Editrix

• **Must I air-dry after a spiritual bath?**

I live in a Northern State and it's winter and quite chilly. Is there any way to avoid or to substitute for air drying when performing a spiritual bath so as not to catch a cold?

—path2success

I'm going to tell you what I tell everyone that tells me something like that. Buy a space heater for your bathroom, they're cheap and a great thing to have.

—Turnsteel

• **Can I shower after a spiritual bath?**

If I take a shower after my spiritual bath, will the bathing effects be negated? Like washing the spell off?

—lmlvr

Definitely don't take a shower right after you do a spiritual bath; it's like washing off all the work you've done to draw something. Physical bath first, then spiritual bath and air dry.

—ConjureMan Ali (M, AIRR)

• **Can I put lotion, perfume, or oils on after a spiritual bath?**

After I'm fully dry from a spiritual bath, can I put lotion on?

—lmlvr

Can I wear perfume, cologne, or scented oils after a spiritual bath?

—coastwitch

Yes. You can put your regular lotion on. You may also consider dosing your lotion with a drop or two of lucky or protective anointing oils. If you enjoy spiritual perfumes like Florida Water or Hoyt's Cologne, feel free to splash them on after the bath. If you are working for a specific goal, such as drawing money or love, you can apply spiritual oils after the bath.

—catherine yronwode (M, AIRR)

• Can I prepare a spiritual bath ahead of time?

I was wondering if it was okay to prepare a bath in advance to actually taking it, not immediately before taking it?

—violet

Yes, you may prepare baths ahead of time and warm them for use. Keep them in the refrigerator to stay freshest. Also, some folks make ice cubes out of them for longer storage. You boil a really concentrated solution, freeze it, pop the cubes out the tray (so you can use it for regular ice) and bag the cubes in the freezer. Just add hot water and there you are!

—catherine yronwode (M, AIRR)

• Does boiling herbs to prepare a spiritual bath smell?

Does boiling the herbs for a spiritual bath give off a very questionable aroma in the air of the house? I'd probably be doing this at night and I don't want the smell of something actually waking people up.

—tom

It smells like an herbal tea to me. There are no synthetic scents added or anything — it's just herbs.

—Devi Spring (M, AIRR)

• How can I bathe if a spiritual bath gives me an allergic reaction?

I took a spiritual bath and I thought it was great, but this morning I woke up with a rash all over my body. It really itches. So if I'm allergic to a certain bath, then what alternatives are there to spiritual bathing?

—Rev Dotson

The first lesson to learn with any bathing product is what Dr. Bronner said: "DILUTE! DILUTE!" In other words, you may have made the bath too strong. We usually use about 1/3 of a packet in a standard 40 - 60 gallon tub or a diluted tea-strength pour-over. Also, you may only be allergic to certain ingredients, in which case choosing a different bath blend would be advised.

—catherine yronwode (M, AIRR)

• Can I use bath crystals to lay tricks rather than to cleanse?

When laying a trick, is it feasible to dissolve bath salts in water, pray over the water, and then sprinkle it on property, spray it on carpets, or leave it in the path of targets? I would like to do this because it'll be less likely than oil to leave a stain and less detectable than sachet powder on some surfaces.
—Lucylookingskyward

Yes, you can use bath crystals dissolved in water to lay a trick. This is a popular way to work with Crossing or Jinx bath crystals, but can also be used to lay love tricks. If you're deploying a wash into someone's foot-tracks or on their property, be aware that repeated applications of salt water, as in bath crystal solutions, can harm or kill plants, so be careful.
—aura (M)

• How many baths can I get per packet?

How many baths can you get out of a packet of bath crystals? Do I pour the whole packet in one bath?
—snake

Just wondering: How many baths can you get out of a package of herbs?
—emdeluxe

Usually one bath or two per packet, depending on your purposes and the amount of water you are using. Pouring baths use far less water than tub baths, so you would need a smaller amount of herbs or bath crystals per bath.
—Literarylioness (M)

You can get one, two, or three baths out of a packet of bath crystals.
—Joseph Magnuson (M)

Well, it depends on the bath product you purchase and how you use it. The herb bath packets state "7-Herb Bath, One Day Supply" and "7-Herb Bath, 7 Day Supply," but you would use less for an herbal foot bath. As for the bath crystals, you can get a few tub baths out of those, generally two or three.
—Papa Newt (M)

• How do I dispose of herbs from a spiritual bath preparation?

How do I properly dispose of the herbs I used in my spiritual bath once they have been steeped and strained? Can I throw the herbs away in the trash, off of my property?

—MarkiMark1776

I prefer to compost herb matter. Doesn't your city have recycling? I thought all the cities have recycling now, you know, for "green waste." Maybe you should check into that. Or place it under a bush somewhere. I mean, why send it to a landfill? That's not good stewardship of the Earth.

— catherine yronwode (M, AIRR)

• What do I do with the bath water from a spiritual bath?

After taking a spiritual bath, do you let the water run down the drain when you're done, or do you collect it and throw it at a crossroads, or is there another way to dispose of it which would be best?

—Bubba

In the old days, before people had plumbing, it was the custom to take a hot bath outdoors in a portable wooden or galvanized tub and to simply pour the water out on the ground by tipping the tub over. You could pour to the East or toward Sunrise to draw in money, love, or luck. You could pour to the West or toward Sunset to remove illness, poverty, or sorrow.

Most folks bathe indoors now, but many of us still like to carry a small symbolic cup of water outdoors and dispose of it, either toward the rising Sun or the setting Sun. It need not be poured out at a crossroads — depending on the kind of job you are doing, you could take it to your yard, a cemetery, a river, a tree — but, retaining some of the methods from when people bathed outdoors, you should dispose of at least a token amount in a ritual manner.

—catherine yronwode (M, AIRR)

You would not want to let the bath water just go down the drain. In hoodoo, we dispose of things, and it is the final step in the work and directs the intentions of the work.

—starsinthesky7 (M)

• Where should I dispose of my bath water?

What does one do when they don't live near or within walking distance of a crossroads at which to take the used bath water and throw towards the Sunrise in the East? How important is it that this step be followed precisely?

—xpoeticmutinyx

Disposal of bath water may be done at various locations, depending on the purpose of the bath. The water (or some portion thereof) may be thrown
• in the home yard;
• at a crossroads, usually with the injunction to not look back;
• toward a tree (usually for things you are trying to get rid of, and usually after doing divination with the tree to see if it will help you);
• at a specified location to bring it into contact with a certain person (for instance, in a lover's path, at your job site, or at a grave site).
The direction in which it is thrown may vary as well, including
• toward the rising Sun (if bathing before dawn for something you are trying to draw in or increase in your life);
• toward the setting Sun (for something you are trying to decrease or remove from your life).
In general, disposing of bath water in the prescribed manner does increase the effectiveness and strength of the work, and finishes it neatly.

On the other hand, there are many situations where it is better to take the spiritual bath, even if you don't have a classical crossroads to work with, than it would be to take no bath at all. If nothing else, you always have the rising or setting Sun.

—Lukianos (M, AIRR)

Here are some yard disposals:
• Pour in the front yard or to the East for new beginnings.
• Pour in the gutter off the property or to the West to remove things.
• Pour in the back yard to keep things under your command.

—catherine yronwode (M, AIRR)

If you live in an apartment, pour at the front door, save a little, and dribble it all the way up the stairs so that the last drops falls on your threshold.

—Dr Johannes (M, AIRR)

• **What is the correct technique when throwing out bath water?**

When disposing of bath water, do you always throw it over your left shoulder, towards the East, regardless of whether it's for taking something away or drawing something in? What about over-your-left-shoulder towards the West for getting rid of something? Or directly in front of you, facing East, to draw something — so that you're looking forward into the rising Sun.

— heartexalted

Some people stand in their yard with their back to the Sun and toss the water over their shoulder or under their armpit toward the Sun. Some people just face the Sun and pitch it forward in their yard.

Some folks tell me that if the bath is for removal of bad conditions, they reverse their position and face the Sun, then throw the water backwards, away from the Sun — but if they are working to draw something good, they will face the Sun and pitch the water forward.

At a crossroads, some folks leave a portion at every corner, while others toss into the center, facing various ways according to the type of job at hand.

There is not one single way that everybody does it. Try it a few ways and you will settle on what works best for the specific job you are doing.

— catherine yronwode (M, AIRR)

• **Can I dispose of bath water while driving?**

Am I able to throw it out of the car, without stopping, over my shoulder?

— Floss71

The tradition of throwing bath water over your shoulder is many generations old, but folks who take spiritual baths in urban environments sometimes collect remnant bathwater in a large plastic cup and then, while driving through a four-way intersection, they will tip the cup out the window, just as if pouring out melted ice from a fast-food drink.

By the way, I've noticed that many people have the impression that all baths must be disposed of at a crossroads, but unless I was cleaning up after really mean work — cursing or killing work — I would content myself with throwing my bathwater away in my own backyard.

— MissMichaele (M, AIRR)

• How do I dispose of water from a love bath?

Do I need to do ritually dispose of water that I used to make a honey bath or sugar scrub for love, even though it's not a cleansing bath?
—Learning719 --

A love bath is still a ritual bath, and we dispose of ritual remains in the traditionally appropriate way. Since you're looking to draw love with this bath, you can throw it into the East as the Sun rises so that your love will be drawn to you.
—Devi Spring (M, AIRR)

• How much water needs to be disposed of?

I am not sure I can even lift a full bucket of water high enough to toss over my left shoulder. Is there a minimum quantity of water required? Can I use less than a bucket or the whole contents of the bath?
—Brida

If you are bathing indoors, you don't need to collect a large bucket of remnant bath water. A cup will do, as a symbolic gesture. If you are actually taking a bucket-bath out of doors, just tip it over on the ground.
—Mama Micki (M)

• Can I dispose of the water for someone else?

How would you wash youngsters or a sick person with a spiritual bath, and how would you collect the water to throw at a crossroads?
—Bubba

If I were washing a bedridden person or child, I would perform the bath using a wash-basin or a supervised tub bath, depending on the person's mobility. After administering the bath, I would get rid of the water for the client. I would collect some of the water in a bottle and throw it out the car window at a busy four way intersection far from where the person lived. This form of disposal harmlessly disperses the disease far and wide into the world.
—Literarylioness (M)

• **Do I dispose of bath water daily or dispose of it only once?**

When taking a 9-Herb Bath for 9 days, do I take the remnant water to the crossroads each day for 9 days or save it and take it only once?
—peggy

When I first took an uncrossing bath, I didn't want that mess inside my house, so I bathed and disposed of my water every day. It is how I was taught and it is worth the effort for me. So now I dispose of all bath water daily.
—ConjureMan Ali (M, AIRR)

• **What if I didn't dispose of the bath water correctly?**

I didn't realise I was supposed to dispose of the water at a crossroads so I did a healing bath and didn't do this part. Should I repeat the bath?
—Bipa

Disposal is an integral part of the conjure work that we do and disposal methods reflect our reasons for taking the bath. You do not need to perform a crossroads disposal unless your intention is to send the energy far and wide. If disposal was not done at all, I'd repeat the process to its completion.
—ConjureMan Ali (M, AIRR)

• **What if when returning from water disposal I looked back?**

I disposed of my bath water at a crossroads while throwing it East. The problem is that I was told to leave the crossroads and not look back, but I totally forgot I wasn't supposed to look back when returning home and so I did. I wasn't trying to demonstrate a lack of faith or doubt or anything. Is this still okay, or should I try to work the spell again?
—The

Well, looking back, especially if you were instructed not to, denotes a lack of concentration when doing the job, even if there wasn't a lack of faith in the work. The spell may still manifest, but probably not fully or with maximum results. I think to be on the safe side, do the spell again.
—starsinthesky7 (M)

- **What's the difference between spiritual soaps and bath crystals?**

So what is the difference between spiritual soaps and bath crystals? Is it a general or specific difference? When do you use a spiritual soap as opposed to a full spiritual bath?

—Sharona22

Bath crystals are used in ritual bathing and are often a combination of salts and a condition oil or a blend of salts, condition oils, and appropriate herbs. Spiritual soaps are soaps that have scents associated with a magical outcome or are manufactured for a specific purpose by companies that make spiritual products.

Typically people use bath crystals when they are taking a ritual bath. This would be considered a more major endeavour than washing with a spiritual soap. It would include significant timing, preparation, time spent in the bath, and proper disposal of the water. Once the work is set in motion by a bath such as this, then some people enjoy using spiritual soaps every day, as a way of keeping the good stuff ongoing.

Spiritual soaps can also be used as a discreet or sneaky way of working on family members and/or business associates, since they usually look much like any other bar of soap. Just pray over the bar as you set it in the bathroom or kitchen of the person or people you wish to affect.

—Miss Bri (M, AIRR)

- **Which is stronger, a spiritual soap or a spiritual wash?**

Between spiritual soaps and spiritual washes, is there one that holds more power than the other or are they both about equal in that regard?

—tnish

I would favor washes over soaps, simply because your intent goes into every single step of preparation. Plus you can completely personalize the ingredients for your cause. When doing a spell or ritual, I would always recommend using a wash. However for day to day maintenance, soaps are great as long as you make sure to use them intentionally and not just soap up with them like you would with a bar of Dial or something.

—Devi Spring (M, AIRR)

• **How do I dispose of the water when using spiritual soaps?**

Although one disposes of used bath water in a crossroads or other appropriate location, if one has been bathing with a spiritual soap like Florida Water Soap, is it necessary to do so as well?
—kevin9

If you are using Florida Water Soap along with prayers, candles, bath crystals, or herbal teas for a spiritual bath, either in preparation for spell work or for blessing or cleansing, then you would dispose of some of the bath water accordingly, in your yard, at a crossroads, or so forth.

If you are simply washing up on a daily basis with Florida Water Soap or any other spiritual soap as "maintenance" or "back-up" work, then you don't have to ritually dispose of the water every time.
—Miss Bri (M, AIRR)

The spiritual soaps are generally used in between more full-fledged rites of bathing or cleansing. When this is the case you do not generally dress in special clothes, light candles, refrain from shaking people's hands, or take your remnant bath water to the crossroads or into the yard, because you are simply "carrying the good work on."
—catherine yronwode (M, AIRR)

• **What is the best timing for the use of spiritual soaps?**

When using spiritual soaps daily, how do you best time washing?
—danger

I usually just use a spiritual soap or body wash whenever I happen to take my daily shower. I say a prayer of intent before scrubbing, but I don't change my schedule to work with a spiritual soap or body wash.
—Devi Spring (M, AIRR)

When using spiritual soaps, I don't follow Moon phases, times, or days, I just use them when I usually wash. They are like a follow-up or back-up to the spell work.
—jwmcclin (M)

• **What's the most effective uncrossing bath?**

Is the 13-Herb Bath more effective or stronger than the Uncrossing Bath Crystals or is there another, better type, such as Jinx Killer? Which is most effective? I need something strong.

—Dimples03

The 13-Herb Bath is neither more nor less "effective" or "strong" than the Uncrossing or Jinx Killer bath crystals. They may be considered complimentary in their use, and best suited for slightly different applications. The 13-Herb Bath is an excellent bath to use for the purpose of removing crossed conditions, obstacles to a cure, stagnant or negative energy, and mental or emotional fog and confusion. Uncrossing Bath Crystals may be used in a similar manner. Jinx Killer Bath Crystals are designed to put an end to specific jinxes or tricks that were laid against you.

That said, both 13-Herb and Uncrossing types of bath are most often done before Sunrise, and will be applied downwards over yourself. Jinx Killer is used similarly, but the bath water may also be poured on the place where someone is known to have laid foot track work against you.

—Lukianos (M, AIRR)

When doing general cleansing baths you can use Uncrossing or 13-Herb baths, as they work on many different cleansing levels. Jinx Killer is to destroy magic that was thrown for you. Hyssop herb works specifically on removing sin — either in the religious sense or as a form of negativity you've brought on yourself. Rue herb works by removing negativity that someone else has put upon you.

When it comes to uncrossing actual conditions, a worker may prescribe very specific herbs for you to bathe in that address the particular ways in which you are crossed. 13-Herb Bath and Uncrossing products cover a lot of ground, with 13-Herb covering even more than the Uncrossing or Jinx Killer products, in my experience.

If you aren't certain what product is best suited to your specific situation, then consider consulting with a professional rootworker who can assess what's going on and suggest the formula most appropriate to your condition. It can ease your mind and ensure the greatest efficacy.

—Devi Spring (M, AIRR)

• How do I cleanse someone who is far away?

How can I cleanse someone I don't have access to or who won't take a spiritual bath?

—sahija

In my experience, for cleansing work to be effective, it has to be performed by or on the person. A worker can help loosen things up, and back up the work that someone is doing on their own behalf, but for results to really take, the person has to do some bathing and washing themselves. Even if I am doing pretty much everything else for a client, I always make them take their own baths and clean their own house.

—Devi Spring (M, AIRR)

You can do healing work and cleansing using a doll baby, but it ought to be backed up in the physical plane with work done by the client or individual, if possible. That isn't to say that if they don't take baths they won't get the effects of the healing or cleansing, but rather it will not be as effective.

—ConjureMan Ali (M, AIRR)

If you need to clean someone to whom you do not have access, or who will or can not do the work, you can baby doll them. I've done this for clients before, and have had good results. Another name for it is healing or cleansing by proxy. You can use proxy methods to work on a target without his or her knowledge, or to cleanse an incarcerated or hospitalized person.

Because you will be bathing the doll, you want to get a plastic baby doll, not a cloth one. They sell them at the craft stores. Ideally you want one where the head and/or arms can be popped off. Stuff the baby doll with Spanish moss and the herbs of the 13-Herb Bath.

If you can't find a plastic baby doll that suits your purpose, you can use a wax doll. Either get a figural candle of the appropriate gender or mold a small beeswax figurine to use as a doll. Load the candle-doll by carving a hole in the bottom, adding herbs, and sealing it with wax, or mold the figurine with appropriate herbs and personal concerns included in the wax.

After preparing the doll, you will name and baptize it for the target. With this, you can do all the baths desired on the baby doll.

—Leah Rivera (M, AIRR)

• **Can I do a Cut and Clear or Black Walnut bath for someone else?**

I am planning on doing the Black Walnut spell and a Cut and Clear spell on behalf of someone else. Can I take the baths myself, or must I have the person I am doing the work for take the baths?

—bluseky

Cut and Clear, and the Black Walnut bath, are a personal matter and in my opinion should be done by the person that wants the results.

—Turnsteel

Bathing by proxy, either on one's own body or by the bathing of dolls that are named to represent a client, is part of our tradition. It's just not all that easy — and these particular baths that you named are ones that most workers feel must be taken by the person who wishes to be cleansed. It would take a very experienced and powerfully focused professional to take a bath for another person by proxy for this type of work — and even then, i doubt it would be half as effective as getting the person to do the work for themselves, even if they were half-scared and 16 years old.

—catherine yronwode (M, AIRR)

• **How often should I cleanse?**

Every month I do a spiritual cleansing. If I did a thorough cleansing two weeks ago but have dealt with an unpleasant situation, should I cleanse right now or can I wait on it, since I will do another full cleansing in two weeks?

—taramia

How often people cleanse is up to them. It's no different than "regular" cleansing. Remember that spiritual cleansing in conjure is tied to physical cleansing. Some people will cleanse regularly and other people will let dirt gather before they cleanse again. The point is that you should cleanse regularly, or if you feel the need, and what that means is up to you and your own situation. If you feel that the situation you have experienced is marking enough that you're asking the question, chances are you should consider a spiritual cleansing even if you're not "on schedule" for it.

—ConjureMan Ali (M, AIRR)

• How do I clean myself after doing negative work?

After doing hot foot work, or crossing someone up, is it okay to simply take a shower with just plain water, and then afterwards air dry and light a white candle anointed with Holy Oil and read a Psalm for cleansing? Can I put Hyssop water in a spray bottle and spray it on my body also?
— Angelina

Well, you probably need more cleansing than that if you're doing crossing or hot foot work on someone. A full spiritual bath using Hyssop or 13-Herb Bath would be best, although in a pinch you can work the Hyssop in a spray bottle as you've described.
— Literarylioness (M)

The usual way to clean yourself up after performing a spell of coercive, crossing, hateful, or cursing magic is to bathe with Hyssop and pray the 51st Psalm. Even a Hyssop spray is more traditional than "just plain water."
— catherine yronwode (M, AIRR)

If you have a bath, take a bath with Hyssop. If you only have a shower, then make a Hyssop tea and bathe with that by pouring it over yourself in the shower just as you would any other spiritual bath.

You can spray yourself with Hyssop and you can also anoint your body with Hyssop oil prepared in an appropriate base like Almond or Olive oil.

Lighting one candle is fine, but often when taking spiritual baths we use two candles, arranged in the bathroom so that you are walking between them, and I especially like this symbolism of going through a symbolic gate fresh and clean after doing harsher work.

You probably also want to pray for forgiveness while you bathe. Psalms 51 is a very traditional choice, due to its mention of Hyssop.
— Miss Bri (M, AIRR)

Lighting some cleansing incense like Uncrossing or Jinx Killer while taking a full cleansing bath would be advisable after doing any crossing work. Consider putting up some protections or reversals after the cleansing bath as well.
— Dr Johannes (M, AIRR)

• **How often do I cleanse when doing negative work?**

How frequently do I need to do cleansing when performing crossing or cursing work?

— mabel

If you will be doing the work over multiple days, it is a good idea to cleanse yourself each day after you have done that day's negative work. A Hyssop bath or similar cleansing is excellent.

—Lukianos (M, AIRR)

One way to work would be to make up a small amount of Hyssop tea and use that to spray your face and wash your hands every day after doing the daily portion of the cursing or crossing. Once the work is completed, then you can clean the work area, or the room in which you did the work, with Chinese Wash and take a spiritual bath for yourself — either with Hyssop herb or 13-Herb Bath — while praying Psalms 51 for forgiveness from sin. This would be a more thorough method of cleansing.

—aura (M)

• **How soon must I cleanse after doing negative work?**

What is the longest I can wait to cleanse myself after laying an enemy trick or working a destructive or negative spell on the altar or at work?

—K54

Hoodoo is a set of folk beliefs, not a set of game rules. How long after you dig in the mud can you walk around before taking a bath? How long after changing the oil on your car can you go before you want to wash up?

Personally, i don't like to walk around in a spiritually unclean state. I want to finish my work by cleaning up afterwards. Your mileage may vary.

If cursing someone from my home, i would clean up at once. If hot-footing someone at the work-place, then i recommend that you carry a small bottle of prepared cleansing tea — such as Hyssop and VanVan or an herbal tea, diluted — and after laying the Hot Foot trick, go into the bathroom and wash your hands and face with the prepared bath-tea.

—catherine yronwode (M, AIRR)

• Must I cleanse if a rootworker is doing the negative work for me?

Do I need cleansing and protection even if a rootworker is actually doing the dark work for me?

—movingmountains

When rootworkers do work on your behalf it is not uncommon that they may have you work in tandem by performing baths, laying out tricks, cleaning your home, and so on and so forth. Regular cleansing and protection is therefore traditional and recommended.

For example, when I work on behalf of a client, I almost always prescribe baths, anointing with oil, cleansing the home, or other tasks that help further the work while clearing out blockages and clearing away anything keeping the desired manifestation from happening.

—ConjureMan Ali (M, AIRR)

Yes, your wish to do harm to someone was why the work was done, you started the chain of events that led to the person being crossed, and thus you need to take a bath in Hyssop and ask the Lord to forgive and cleanse you of your sins.

—Turnsteel

The tradition is that if you curse someone, even if you hire someone to do it for you, then you should get right with God by taking a Hyssop bath and reciting the 51st Psalm.

—catherine yronwode (M, AIRR)

• Do I need a spiritual house cleansing after doing negative work?

When doing dark work, I use Chinese Wash to cleanse the area that I'm working in. Do I need to do the whole house?

—lilavenger

I don't clean the whole house, just the area where I'm working, for what it's worth. I use Chinese Wash. I do clean up IMMEDIATELY afterward, though, and then i take a Hyssop bath and say Psalms 51.

—catherine yronwode (M, AIRR)

• What if I don't cleanse when doing negative work?

Say you do dark or negative work or cursing spells and don't cleanse yourself afterwards: What would happen? If you are doing bad works, wouldn't being angry and hateful and full of the work be stronger and therefore something that you would not want to cleanse off of yourself?
— wraithklewn

I suppose it would depend on your moral sensibilities. If you like walking around dirty, then go for it.

However, i will note, based on my experience as a practitioner, that:
• Those who intend to stay "angry and hateful" (your words) tend to become obsessed with the negative aspects of life in general, and not only do they get sucked into the continual performance of hostile magic, their outer lives tend to attract hostility, anger, and hatefulness.
• Conjure is primarily a Judeo-Christian form of folk magic, which means that most of us want to get right with God.

I advise against trying to rewrite or undermine the moral basis of the living folk-magical tradition of hoodoo; instead i advise you to enter fully and gladly into the Christian culture from which it sprang.
— catherine yronwode (M, AIRR)

I've found that not cleansing after "dark" work can have several effects, including a few really noticeable ones that many people report:
• If you are doing dark work, then try working love or money spells, you'll track that dark, chaotic energy with you into the good work.
• People who have any sensitivity will sense the dirt that accumulates on you spiritually. This may also start affecting your normal life: More fights, more arguments in your life, and more issues at home will result.
• There *is* a record of people literally getting sick from performing dark work. If you don't cleanse properly there is a chance that you'll physically expose yourself.
• The spiritual bath is not only a powerful spiritual experience, but a psychological one too; it helps you let go of dark emotions, obsessive feelings, and constant anger that can be detrimental.

The point is: Cleanse!
— ConjureMan Ali (M, AIRR)

• Will spiritual cleansing remove good spell work?

I know spiritual cleansing is used to get rid of the bad stuff someone has put on us. But what if we have done good spells like Crown of Success or Blessing: Will that also be removed?

—path2success

I get this question a lot from clients who are asking for spiritual cleansing or who need to cleanse their homes: "If I use this product will it clear out all the good spirits and energies too?" I tell them that it will not, but I am not really sure. Just wondering what the actual answer to that is.

—Maya

The fearfulness with which some newcomers to hoodoo approach the work — and i will go further here and say that most of them are white and not from the traditional US South — is sad. I feel sorry for their fearfulness, which at times verges on OCD contamination phobias, but all i can do is say to them that their attitudes come from a different culture, not the one in which conjure developed.

The cleansing baths and washes we use in hoodoo selectively target and wipe out curses, negative energy, and bad luck. In conjure culture, the terms used for that form of negativity would include evil messes, jinxes, enemy rootwork, or anything physically thrown with the intention of causing crossed conditions.

Not only that, the user who was raised in conjure culture will have learned as a youngster how to pray while cleansing, and will know that the prayers will be for the bad to be gone and the good to be enhanced. The 23rd Psalm is one usual choice — and it is not a prayer that will send away angels or guardian spirits. On the contrary, it grants abundance while it fosters wisdom, protection, and guidance.

Try to work with clients and customers who are new to hoodoo by reassuring them that they have entered into a world of long-standing Southern family spiritual traditions, not some freaky wild-energy-teen-witchcraft movie. The work does what we intend it to do, nothing more nothing less. State your intentions clearly, pray over your bathing and cleaning water, and don't obsess about things going wrong.

—catherine yronwode (M, AIRR)

• Can I time my baths using planetary hours?

I am wondering if the spiritual bath would retain its worth if performed during other times than Sunrise. For example, what if I would like to align a bath to certain planetary hours?

—Frater Hod

In the traditions of conjure, as I learned them, the taking of a spiritual bath for cleansing or for drawing helpful things usually takes place with the dawn. There are other times when one would take ritual baths, and the hour or timing of the bath is not as important. For example, after performing a curse on someone, one would cleanse oneself of the evil act with a Hyssop bath. Folks don't specify when it should be performed, other than after you are finished, you should immediately go and cleanse yourself.

As there are a number of conjure folk who do follow magical timing by the weeks, days, planetary hours, Moon cycles, and such when doing their magical work, and the ritual bath is part of such magical work, I don't see why you couldn't time your magical bath for certain planetary hours that are conducive to your goal, using the appropriate bath products.

—Christopher Lung

• What's the best timing for a love bath?

My boyfriend and I have a date planned this coming Friday. I want our date to be very romantic. I want to take a spiritual bath before our date using Come to Me or Love Me bath crystals. I want to know, is it best for me to take it that morning or should I take it a few hours before our date?

—danger

Take it soon before the date, so that the scent remains on your body.

—catherine yronwode (M, AIRR)

If you absolutely have to take the bath in the morning and can't wait until right before the date, then keep a bit of your used bath water in a small spray bottle, add a couple of drops of condition oil, shake it up, and use as a perfume.

—aura (M)

• **What's the best timing for a spiritual cleansing bath?**

For a cleansing bath, what time, day of the week, and Moon phase are best to obtain good results?

—sahija

Most baths of cleansing are performed at the time of dawn. The waning Moon is a good time to remove bad conditions; the waxing Moon brings good tidings. The day can be Sunday for blessings and health.

—catherine yronwode (M, AIRR)

• **Is it okay to bathe at night rather than at dawn?**

Is there any consensus on whether spiritual baths need to be done late at night before going to bed or very early in the morning after waking? I understand that from Midnight to 6:00 AM is when they should be done in hoodoo. I ask because I was raised in a house with very specific ideas about being "clean" and having everything "clean" before sleeping, so it feels "right" for me to do the bath and dispose of the water before going to bed rather than waiting until I wake up.

—Maljen

There are no magical police that are going to come to your house and arrest you for taking your cleansing baths before bed.

Other traditions have different timing and instructions for making and taking baths — however, in hoodoo; spiritual bathing to cleanse and for most purposes is done just prior to the rising of the Sun.

—Devi Spring (M, AIRR)

Either you wish to follow our traditions or not. Our traditions are firmly, deeply ("consensus-wise") committed to bathing "soon in the morning," AT SUNRISE. You know, as Devi said, "there are no hoodoo police," but, also, as Ken Kesey said, "You're either ON the bus or OFF the bus." Thanks for considering that this is not a make-it-up-and-do-what-feels-good tradition, but a living, culturally defined, respected tradition with a very long history which it is not your place to remake in your own image.

—catherine yronwode (M, AIRR)

• Must I take the spiritual bath before dawn?

Does it make a difference if I take a bath at my regular time instead of at dawn as suggested?

—miamore

I prefer to bathe in the morning just as the Sun comes up. This is an old, old-time ritual and that's the way it has always been done, going all the way back to Africa. Try to work with these teachings the way they were passed down for thousands of years before you decide to change them.

—catherine yronwode (M, AIRR)

You should follow the timing which was suggested to you if you want to do things right. Keep in mind that the timing was suggested to you for a specific reason, not just to make the bath more difficult.

—Devi Spring (M, AIRR)

To bathe at sunrise, and take the bathwater (or a portion) to the crossroads and/or pour it to the East are not arbitrary details in hoodoo bathing practice. These elements are an integral part of the tradition, and very, very old. Some say they may go back past the Middle Passage to Africa, with the emphasis on the Sunrise being a reference to the old worship of the Sun. In like manner offering the bathwater to the crossroads may very well go back to the ancient African customs of pouring out libations to the crossroads spirit. Since the bath rite is similar in many ways (including its emphasis on Sunrise) to Jewish ritual baths, some have speculated that both the hoodoo rite and the Jewish rite go back to ancient Egypt. In any event, when you follow the hoodoo bath rite according to its tradition, you are participating in a very ancient custom. And, if you follow the rite as it is traditionally observed, then you are also helping in the preservation of that rite.

Think about it: This ritual survived slavery. That's pretty amazing!

So, to make a long story short, if you're going make changes to something this old, with this much meaning in all its parts, then it better be for a really good reason, and not just because of a desire to not be personally inconvenienced.

—Jibrael

• Should cleansing baths be taken before and after all spell-work?

Before and after doing a spell, should I cleanse myself?
—Bella06

It isn't always necessary to bathe before spellwork. Some spells ask for you to do this, and others do not. Additionally, if you're confused, flustered or otherwise unfocused, you could certainly start with a Clarity bath.
—MissMichaele (M, AIRR)

Don't cleanse after spells for drawing, like Love Me, Fast Luck, Healing, Money Drawing, House Blessing, Court Case, Wealthy Way, Look Me Over, Lucky Number, or Crown of Success. You want to keep what you did on you.

Don't cleanse after spells of removal, reversal, or protection, because the Jinx Killer, Uncrossing, Fiery Wall of Protection, or Reversing spell is also a cleansing trick, so cleansing would be redundant.

Do clean up after working negative tricks against others, like Hot Foot, Destruction, Break-Up, Jinx, or Damnation. The cleansing is to take off your own sin if, God forbid, you erred by making a wrongful accusation or calling down an unjust curse on the head of an innocent person.
—catherine yronwode (M, AIRR)

• Must the 13-Herb bath be done for thirteen days?

Must I do 13-Herb Baths for thirteen days, or will a one-day bath, Chinese Wash, and burning Frankincense be enough to rid myself of bad luck?
—MarkiMark1776

Taking a 13-Herb bath for thirteen days is not a requirement. You can periodically do just one such bath, as a form of spiritual "freshening up."

As a young woman, i was told to do it once — but i also heard practitioners tell others to do it three times or thirteen times.

The reason for the variation was the practitioner's spiritual understanding of the degree of problems that the client had. In other words, if the client had an average amount of need for spiritual cleaning, then a one-time bath was prescribed, and the stronger the problem, the more baths were prescribed.
—catherine yronwode (M, AIRR)

• How often are the special herb baths taken?

I would like advice on how often to take the 13-Herb, 9-Herb, and 7-Herb baths — once a month, twice a year? I understand the importance of taking them periodically, but I would like advice on the frequency.
—jwmcclin (M)

Frequency of bathing will depend on an individual's personal situation and needs. Some folks need a single 13-Herb Bath a few times a year to cut through whatever spiritual crud they may encounter going through life. Other folks are magnets to trouble, or live in areas with high concentrations of trouble, or may be unfortunate enough to attract the enmity of someone with the ability to do ongoing negative work on them. For the latter, a series of thirteen daily 13-Herb baths, followed by weekly 13-Herb Baths thereafter, may be what they need to keep themselves free of negativity and bad luck.

9-Herb Baths are often taken in a series of nine daily baths in support of personal mastery or success work. They are also taken on as-needed basis by card readers, seers, and psychics to heighten insight and accuracy.

Along a similar line, those who gamble a lot may want to take 7-Herb Baths on a regular basis, perhaps every seven days, as part of their overall preparation for going out to gamble. They may also use the Gambler's Gold Lucky 7 Hand Wash herbs in a similar way.

In all of these cases, the type of bath and the frequency is determined by the kinds of things that the person is doing in his or her life, as well as his or her susceptibility to environmental and social factors.
—Lukianos (M, AIRR)

• Should I repeat the same bath twice or combine two baths?

Should the same bath be taken multiple times, like a few days in a row, or is an appropriate combination of two different baths a better choice?
—JasmineTalula

A divination, performed by yourself or by a reader, can let you know how many days are indicated for the best results, as well as if a combination of bath crystals will work better than a single formula in your specific case.
—Devi Spring (M, AIRR)

• Can bath crystals be combined?

Can we combine multiple bath crystals — such as Love Me, Money Drawing, and Fast Luck — so only one wash is necessary for either bathing or house cleaning?

—path2success

Yes, you can combine bath crystals in the way that you have described. Just make sure that you are clear about what you want to accomplish before you start combining ingredients.

—Miss Bri (M, AIRR)

• Can I use remnant water from a personal bath in house cleaning?

I want to take a 13-Herb Bath and follow with a house cleaning using Chinese Wash, but I am questioning the addition of my bath water to the house wash. Both of these would have "bad" stuff from me in the water yet they are both considered a spiritual cleansing. Is it necessary to do a separate spiritual cleansing bath after my 13-Herb Bath for uncrossing?

—sephirah

You do not need to take two cleansing baths, because 13-Herb Bath is both a spiritual cleansing bath and a jinx-removing bath in one. You can safely include some of your own remnant bath water from the 13-Herb Bath (or freshly-made 13-Herb bath-tea) in the Chinese Wash water you use to scrub out your space, because 13-Herb Bath is a versatile mix, suitable for both heavy-duty personal spiritual cleansing and for house cleaning.

Often, cleansing spiritual work has two phases:

First, remove any jinxes or obstacles by cleaning yourself and your space thoroughly (washing down from head to toes with 13-Herb Bath, and washing the house top to bottom and back to front with Chinese Wash).

Second, draw in what is desired, like peace, money, love, or protection. You can take a second bath (washing upwards from feet to head with luck-drawing products) and wash your space a second time (front to back), or you can omit the second bath and the second floor-wash and just scrub the entrance with a drawing wash.

—Lukianos (M, AIRR)

BIBLIOGRAPHY

Balch, Phyllis A. Prescription for Herbal Healing. Avery Trade. 2002.

Betz, Hans Dieter. Greek Magical Papyri in Translation, Including the Demotic Spells. University of Chicago Press, 1986.

Casas, Starr. Working the Root: the Conjure Workbook, Vol. 1. Pendraig Publishing, 2013.

Cunningham, Scott and David Harrington. The Magical Household. Llewellyn Publications, 1983.

Dillaire, Claudia. Egyptian Revenge Spells: Anchient Rituals for Modern Payback. Ten Speed Press, 2009.

Gladstar, Rosemary. Herbal Healing for Women: Simple Home Remedies for Women of All Ages. Simon & Shuster Inc., 1993.

Green, James. The Herbal Medicine-Maker's Handbook: A Home Manual. Crossing Press, 2000.

Hyatt, Harry Middleton. Hoodoo – Conjuration – Witchcraft – Rootwork. [Five Vols.] Memoirs of the Alma Egan Hyatt Foundation, 1970-1978.

Long, Carolyn Morrow. Spiritual Merchants: Religion, Magic, and Commerce. University of Tennessee Press, 2001.

Malbrough, Ray T. The Magical Power of the Saints: Evocations and Candle Rituals. Llewellyn Publications, 1998.

McQuillar, Tayannah Lee. Rootwork: Using the Folk Magick of Black America for Love, Money, and Success. Fireside Books, 2003.

Michaele, Miss and Prof. Charles Porterfield. Hoodoo Bible Magic: Sacred Secrets of Scriptural Sorcery. Missionary Independent Spiritual Church, 2014.

Mickaharic, Draja. Spiritual Cleansing. Samuel Weiser, 1982.

Millett, Deacon. Hoodoo Honey and Sugar Spells: Sweet Love Magic in the Conjure Tradition. Lucky Mojo Curio Co., 2013.

Slonim, Rivkah. Total Immersion: A Mikvah Anthology. Jason Aronson, 1996.

Trachtenburg, Joshua. Jewish Magic and Superstition: A Study in Folk Religion. Behrman's Jewish Book House, 1939.

Tierra, Michael. The Way of Herbs. Pocket Books, 1980.

yronwode, catherine. The Art of Hoodoo Candle Magic in Rootwork, Conjure, and Spiritual Church Services. Missionary Independent Spiritual Church, 2013.

yronwode, catherine et al. The Black Folder: Personal Communications on the Mastery of Hoodoo. Missionary Independent Spiritual Church, 2013.

yronwode, catherine. Hoodoo Herb and Root Magic: A Materia Magica of African-American Conjure. Lucky Mojo Curio Co., 2002.

yronwode, catherine. Hoodoo Rootwork Correspondence Course: A One-Year Series of Weekly Lectures in African American Conjure. Lucky Mojo Curio Co., 2006.